Sandi is an insightful writer—she helps her cl
their complex businesses into clear, concise te
understands the important role that media cc
organization's ability to grow and thrive in today's economy. Her
understanding and insiders knowledge of the new business is
superb! Sandi is a sure bet in today's uncertain world.

> — **Jan Edwards**
> Principal/CEO Red Arrows Consulting

PR today is all about—a combination of getting the message
right, and delivering it to the right audience at the right time. As
a former marketer and TV station general manager, Sandi is
uniquely positioned to understand both sides of the PR effort—
the publicists' and the journalists'. Combine that with her lively
and witty writing style and you can't go wrong!

> — **Maryann Baldwin**
> Vice President, Magid Media Futures
> Frank N. Magid Associates

Short of getting on Oprah, following Sandi Gehring's advice is
your best bet for getting favorable publicity. Professional,
prompt, and passionate, Sandi knows broadcast media inside out,
and she works her heart out making sure her clients look good. If
you get a change to hire her, grab it, and if you're serious about
publicizing your business, make sure you read her book.

> — **Roy Rasmussen**, coauthor
> *Publishing for Publicity: How to Promote*
> *Your Business with a Book*

One of the hardest parts of making any venture a success can be getting the word out and Sandi Gehring knows how to do that at the highest levels! From crafting an effective message to knowing how to work with production and print, her insights and experience have been crucial to successfully marketing our message to the national audience. This book is a must-read for anyone wanting insight into how the media works and how to get your message across.

> — **Tim Wilkins**
> Nationally-syndicated Debt Specialist,
> Debtpoint.com

An expert in broadcast promotion and television news, Sandi Yost Gehring combines rich media experience with solid messaging research, and delivers a clear guide to turning media coverage into great publicity. This is a Òmust readÓ for anyone who is trying to get a message heard in today's frenetic, fractured media landscape!

> — **Barbara Hamm Lee**
> Executive Producer/Host, *Another View*,
> WHRO Public Media

Breaking Your Own News

Using the Media to Spread Your
Message and Grow Your Business!

by
SANDRA GEHRING

PUBLICITY PRESS

©2011 Sandra Gehring

All rights reserved. No part of this book may be reproduced or transmitted in any form or by any means, electronic or mechanical, including photo-copying, recording, or by any information storage or retrieval system with-out written permission from Sandra Gehring and Publicity Press, except for the inclusion of brief quotations in a review.

Book design by Marian Hartsough
Cover design by Michael Tanamachi and Marian Hartsough

Disclaimer: This book is intended to provide information only, and should not be construed as professional business or financial advice. No income claims are stated or implied. How you put this information to use is up to you.

ISBN-10: 1-932311-58-0
ISBN-13: 978-1-932311-58-7

Printed in the United States of America

PUBLICITY PRESS
1285 Stratford Avenue, Suite G262
Dixon, California 95620
866-221-8408
http://www.breakingyourownnews.com

Contents

Introduction

- Publicity: Who wants it?
- Who needs it?
- Who gets it?
- Who cares?

Many of us watch the news and wonder how Joe Schmoe got his mug on camera. Haven't you ever wondered how the press finds these so-called "experts"? Other people are asked the questions that you deal with professionally every day. Why is that? You could answer those same reporter questions in your sleep, perhaps more accurately—and you'd like that kind of free exposure too. Is that just the luck of the draw? The answer is "No." Do they know something you don't know? The answer to that one is, "Yes!"

Sometimes not getting any attention in the media though, isn't entirely bad. Although Joe Schmoe really does seem to be a camera hog, on the other hand we've also seen the intrepid television reporter chasing some hapless business owner into his house, while shouting, "But Mr. Doofus, didn't you know your staff was ripping off your customers?" Ouch! Obviously this is NOT the kind of exposure that anyone wants, and aren't you glad you don't have that kind of media attention? Again, the answer is "yes."

So this is the yin and yang of media coverage in today's incredibly electronic and plugged-in world. You can't figure out how to get publicity for yourself, while some other people seem to have already mastered it. And you want that positive attention. There are other times when deep down you may be secretly glad that you don't have any media coverage. The reality is that if you own your own business, are in business for yourself, or want to have a growing practice, YOU need publicity. Keeping yourself and your skills under the proverbial bushel basket won't get you any customers, it won't make the phone or cash register ring, and it won't build your reputation.

Media exposure and publicity is a powerful weapon, regardless of your profession or your business. Our savvy Joe Schmoe has managed to get himself on the receiving end of great press, and that positions him very well competitively. The media coverage for and about him means that Joe is now perceived as having an expertise that other people do not have. This expertise or so-called credibility makes Joe and his business more valuable to potential customers.

When it comes to potential, the media today is full of opportunities, and legitimate publicity can help position you in a positive light. The glow of great press can grow your bottom line. As the communication environment becomes more cluttered with ads, and consumers are bombarded with non-stop commercial messages, media coverage can set you and your business apart. The right publicity, done correctly, done quickly, and done at the right moment can position you as an "expert in your field."

But what is the "right publicity?" The right publicity and the kind of media attention that you should want is exactly the kind of coverage that Joe Schmoe gets. You do not want the kind of media exposure that poor Mr. Doofus got . . . well, duh!?! But how does that happen? Did Joe just win the public relations lottery? Nope. Joe benefited from some great media placement, because he knew how to strike, what to propose, who to contact, and what the media wants. This is work that keeps public relations firms in business.

But hiring a public relations company is costly, and without them it seems that the press only comes knocking on your door when the news is bad. . .right? It can be hard to market yourself effectively to the media, but for those who manage to do so, it is possible to join the ranks of the regularly-called-upon professionals and earn the credibility and reputation that will set both you and your service apart.

Our boy Joe Schmoe has figured out how to use media coverage to his advantage. Who else will benefit from media coverage and from this book?

If you run a business, own a small business, or are in business for yourself, you will benefit from this book.

If you are in a professional service firm (you know: doctors, dentists, attorneys, realtors, consultants, financial services, software developers, career counselors, educators, and many more), you will learn from this book.

If you toil away in the important but often anonymous world of non-profit organizations, you need this book.

The right media exposure can mean good things for you and your business, and as luck would have it, there are scores of books, websites, and seminars about publicity and media coverage. And I do mean scores. But there is a barrier to your media exposure solution: these PR books, articles, blogs, and websites were written by experts don't have any actual media experience. This book is different than most, because it is written by a media insider and not by a PR person. Nothing against the typical PR types, but in my opinion *they are to media what exterminators are to your ant infestation: you want the service the exterminator can provide but at the same time you really feel like you ought to be able to do it yourself.*

I have good news for you though: with my help and with this book, you can handle getting media exposure for yourself. The world of public relations views media exposure as a battle. But publicity is not a fight, it is an intelligent partnership. It has rules and regulations all its own—rules that the people inside the media can cite in their sleep. This book will school you in the rules that media people like to keep to themselves.

This book deciphers the code about who get positive press coverage and who gets no coverage or even negative coverage. This real world advice is written by a twenty-five-year news media professional with experience at CNN, NBC and the *New York Times*. I have toiled mightily in the print media, local television, cable television and national news shows. And actually I loved the work, loved the media, loved being inside the media. My years of being in front of the camera, more years behind the camera, and then ultimately writing for the news cameras, have taught me a virtual Top Ten list of media coverage benefits.

I am the rare breed of professional publicists who did not flunk out of the media profession. I managed a successful and wide-ranging media career and have chosen now to work with a small group of clients who need publicity. I'm happy to share the secrets I've learned along the way. So buckle your seat belt, because we will be breaking down the tips, tricks and the insider secrets that the media never shares.

I loved writing this book and hope that you will find it helpful for getting media coverage of your business. If there is anything I can help you with, please don't hesitate to contact me.

Sandra Gehring   October 1, 2010
email: gehring123@gmail.com
www.sandragehring.com

Chapter 1

The Prep Work

- What Is Media Coverage in Today's Environment?
- What Has Changed?
- How Does Media Coverage Work?
- Top Ten Reasons Publicity Will Help You
- No News Is Good News

"Everyone has inside of him a piece of good news. The good news is that you don't know how great you can be! What you can accomplish! And what your potential is!"

—Anne Frank

The inspirational young Anne Frank's words are a very good place to start. You **do** have good news, interesting news to share and news that deserves some valuable media coverage. So let's get started on making that happen.

What Is Media Coverage in Today's Environment?

Media coverage today can be a radio interview, a television interview, a TV or radio story without an interview, newspaper or magazine articles, even social media. And although there have been some significant changes, the basics of getting media attention are still the same as they were 25 years ago. The difference today is that there are so many more tools to help generate that attention. Media coverage happens because one of these two things has also happened:

- a news event has occurred and the news media covers the story
- a news story has been proposed and the news media agrees to cover that story

Okay, okay, that may be a no-brainer. It probably goes without saying that as the *Breaking Your Own News* title implies, your sweet spot is in that second category! The news story proposal itself is the stuff of books, websites, articles, PR budgets, and teams of people . . . but it doesn't have to be. Between my experience and your brains we can make strong successful news story proposals happen for you!

Life moves fast and media coverage in the current environment moves at a much faster pace than even a decade ago. Assignment editors, reporters, producers across all local and national news media have access to tons of information and more people to interview than ever before—thanks to savvy social media users, search engines, and assorted mobile devices.

According to Gail Sideman, who runs a publicity firm in Milwaukee, "The speed at which news travels today as compared to five to ten years ago is mind-boggling. There is no set news cycle anymore. It's always on." The opportunity to get media exposure today is more plentiful as well as more challenging. One big downside of trying to get publicity today is that media outlets are dramatically downsized.

Ten years ago a media outlet had more "feet on the street"—or in other words more reporters, more producers, and more writers—than they do today. Bigger news reporting staffs meant that reporters had more time to consider a variety of story proposals.

Some reporters even had time to conduct extra interviews that never saw the light of broadcast or print because they just didn't gel. Media types refer to those as "the good old days" because they are long gone. Gone is the time for thoughtful contemplation and long, lengthy potential interviews.

Here is one telling example from my own backyard: in September 2010 the *Orlando Sentinel*'s top editor announced her retirement. When she took over as editor in 2004, the newsroom staff numbered 340 people. When she retired in October 2010, there were 170 staffers, or about half of the newsroom staff compared to only six years ago.

The new reality for the media is an always-looming deadline, so there is not a moment or resource to be squandered with a news story that might not be strong enough for the newscast or the morning edition. This reality trickles down to your publicity efforts, because the chance of a news media organization having someone available to come out to cover your story is even more unlikely.

What Has Changed and What Hasn't?

The great news for us though is that despite the dramatic downsizing, some things about media coverage have not changed. The most important and consistent element is that you must have a newsworthy story or "hook" to help garner attention for you or your business. You must write well, communicate clearly, and know who to contact at each media source (for example, you don't send information for the latest tech gadget to the food editor). We will review this process step by step in the following chapters.

Here is a media coverage evolution and timeline:

Ten years ago:

- it was still easy to call your contacts in the media outlets directly and talk to them about your story

- media people had more time and interest in listening to why you and your business were publicity worthy
- if your subject was about the Internet or biotech it was easy to get it in print without a lot of effort
- Even with the greater numbers of news media personnel available, some businesses spent thousands of dollars to secure publicity

Five years ago:

- the media game started to change
- as the economy became more difficult, news media budgets were slashed
- budget cuts meant fewer reporters and fewer writers
- the remaining reporters were under severe time pressure to meet looming deadlines for broadcast or print
- finding a media person to listen to any story pitch became harder and harder

Today:

- you need to be savvier about current trends if you hope to crack the media coverage code
- there are more opportunities to publicize yourself for virtually no cost
- you can do it yourself more readily if you understand who your audience is and how they gather information
- online media outlets have increased the number of venues you can utilize for your story
- the 24-hour news cycle of cable/satellite television and the Internet has given more people a better than average chance of being covered
- some of the "reporters" today are really laypeople with a blog and an audience of followers

- the 24-hour news cycle means that you have to move faster in getting the word out to capitalize on big news events

Lisa Douglas owns a boutique public relations agency based in Atlanta, Georgia. She has been in the public relations and marketing industry for twenty years and has seen the changes caused by the passage of time, budgets, and new technologies. Lisa says all of the changes are both good news and bad news for individuals and businesses. Lisa explains, "The advent of Internet usage to get the word out about your product or service has leveled the playing field for most small and micro businesses." This means your ability to contact the media via email, to send an immediate electronic media "alert," and even to use social media to increase your profile is much better than in the past. This book is designed to help you meet the challenges of media coverage today.

How Does Media Coverage Work?

For our purposes, the term "media coverage" is comparable to publicity and public relations. Publicity is sometimes referred to as "free advertising." As a PR pro I don't ever refer to publicity as "free" because it actually takes a lot of hard work. But if it isn't "free advertising" then what is it? This is a good time to get some definitions out on the table so here goes:

Publicity is: *information with news value that is used as a means of gaining public attention or support. The subjects of publicity include people (for example, politicians and performing artists), goods and services, organizations of all kinds, and works of art or entertainment. Among other things, publicity-driven-exposure sends a simultaneous message to many people. This instant messaging benefits the recipient in a variety of ways.*

A publicist is: *a person whose job is to generate and manage publicity for a product, public figure (especially a celebrity), for a band, or for a work such as a book or movie. Publicists sometimes work at large companies handling multiple clients.*

Media refers to: *various means of communication. For example, television, radio, and the newspaper are different types of media. "Media" can also be used to describe the press or news reporting agencies.*

News media refers specifically to: *the mass media that focuses on presenting current news to the public. These include print media (newspapers, magazines), broadcast media (radio stations, television stations, television networks), and now some Internet-based options.*

Mass media denotes: *a section of the media specifically designed to reach a large audience. The term was coined in the 1920s with the advent of nationwide radio networks, mass-circulation newspapers, and magazines.*

Just for reference: the person who hopes for publicity cannot always wait around for the news to present opportunities. They must also try to create their own news, or a story that is newsworthy. If you've done any checking, you probably already know that most of the websites, books and articles about publicity have been written by the publicists. This is important, because good as publicists may be, they can cost you money.

Even if you spend all the money in the world, I can tell you as a former media insider that not everything the PR brethren counsel is to your benefit. After all, publicists are in business to make money too. I work as a publicist and only take on a few clients at a time—not because I'm "rolling in dough," but because securing good publicity takes a lot of time and attention. The next chapters will explain in detail exactly how you can put my experience to work for you!

Let's revisit that whole "publicity as free advertising" concept just once more. When you compare buying advertising to receiving publicity, the obvious advantages of publicity are lower cost and higher **credibility**. In our plugged-in world, many people are suspicious of commercials. Consumers feel that the advertisers will say or do almost anything to sell a product. This belief may not be warranted, but it does create a great opportunity for good publicity. Those same people who are suspicious of commercials feel that if something is covered by the media as an informational news story, it must be true!

Our definition of publicity mentioned that media coverage can really benefit the recipient in many ways. Ten ways, as a matter of fact—take a look:

Top Ten Reasons Publicity Will Help You

When it comes to publicity, one big benefit to you is that media coverage is the chance to reach large audiences. In the spirit of media superstar David Letterman and his infamous nightly Top Ten list, let's review what every media professional knows that news coverage can do for you:

1. powerfully and quickly help to develop a positive image for you
2. organically and naturally create strong awareness of your company's products or services
3. economically provide the equivalent of a million dollars worth of paid advertising
4. act as a credibility builder (studies show that media coverage is five times more believable than advertising)
5. increase visibility in your market by cost-effectively promoting you to customers and potential customers
6. increase visibility in your own industry by giving you the advantage over competitors who do not "get it"
7. generate leads (the right kind of publicity can turn an ordinary company into a booming business)
8. position you as expert in your field

9. create brand reinforcement by increasing the perception that you are active and "on the move"
10. build morale

I particularly like Number Ten because it is a little known secret. Why? The battle to recruit the best possible staff will be the next great challenge for all business. People who work with you want to feel proud of where they work. The more your staff sees your own positive publicity, the more it justifies their decision that they are working for a fabulous company. . .yours! Just one more reason not to underestimate the power of good PR when attracting a new workforce and retaining existing staff.

It should be pretty clear that news coverage is obviously beneficial, but news coverage is also not-so-obviously a fluid concept. Why is that? Because in our press and publicity efforts:

No News is Good News

This is the first really important aspect to master so get your highlighter out:

> *Your ability to generate media coverage is greater if no other big news is occurring at the same time.*

In the media an important news story or event is referred to as a **"big story."** The absence of any big story is called a "slow news day." If you contact the media with a potential story it could be perfectly viable for a slow news day but that same potential story will be ignored in the face of a big story.

What exactly is a big story? Examples should be obvious if you own a television set, and some have probably already come to mind. The local media considers big stories to include:

- shootings
- multiple vehicle car crashes
- armed robberies

- missing children
- large fires
- high profile court cases
- manhunts
- murders
- any new scandal
- ALL severe weather

We may not agree that all of these things *should* constitute big news. But agree or not, it is the reality of local media and local media coverage. You can trust the fact that news stories like these make news directors salivate, which translates to immediate reporting assignments for nearly the entire newsroom.

To be fair, my friends in the media are not necessarily happy when bad things happen. But there is a certain "this is why we became news people" mentality that kicks in during big news. In most cities these kinds of big stories don't occur all that often. The other reality is that you and I have absolutely no control over any of the **big news** variables.

On a national level **big news** means any larger versions of the stories above PLUS:

- elections
- political scandals
- natural disasters
- terrorism
- serial killers
- financial scandals
- celebrity scandals

The national news tends to be is a little scandal heavy. Sad but true. This is how the news media operates in the first part of the twenty-first century. Big news is always worthy of airtime, and of column inches in the paper. Not exactly a V-8 moment for any of us. But most days, thankfully, there is not any big news. Most days in the life of the news media are "slow news days." You are about to learn why this is your own media coverage sweet spot.

This book will include good information about utilizing the print media, but is intended to have the largest focus on the electronic media. The simple reason for this is that the electronic media can deliver a bigger bang for your buck. Readership of local print publications has been on the decline for years. Print media coverage can still be helpful of course, but I'm a big believer in the old adage of "fishing where the fish are." In other words, let's focus our attention on the things that will get the message out to more people in the most efficient manner . . . which is TV and radio.

Most people who are starting out to secure media coverage and reading this book should test the waters locally before running with the big dogs on a national basis. There will be times though that coverage in the national media will be of interest to you and your story will be of interest to them. The good news is that all of the same basic principles apply. *Breaking Your Own News* is a very scalable approach!

Media coverage always starts with a story. The rapidly-changing media environment puts increasing pressure on the process of putting together an appetizing news story proposal . . . so settle in and get ready for your first taste of the news story proposal process.

Chapter 2

Throw Caution to the Wind and Get FAT!

- The FAT Theory
- Focused
- Attention Getting
- Timely
- Ask Not What the Media Can Do for You, Ask What You Can Do for the Media
- Why Standard Press Releases Are Prehistoric

"Publicity can be terrible. But only if you don't have any."

—Jane Russell

If you have been hungering for some positive attention from the media, or thirsting for some of that "free advertising," you can now officially join legions of other businesses, large and small, who want the same thing. You want to be noticed, even applauded, for your latest acquisition, hire, merger, community outreach, fund raiser, business growth, new idea, and your particular expertise. And you can be!

But so far, this has probably proven to be much easier said than done. Although your story may not be the biggest news ever, you believe that it is worthy of **some** coverage **somewhere**, but the problem is how to make that happen. Haven't you wondered how the news media pick out the stories that they do cover?

Because you are a smart professional, you have already correctly calculated that media coverage helps business people be perceived as "experts." If you are seen on the news giving good ideas or information, you can come across to readers or viewers as a friend giving some great tips. We will review in greater detail that there is nothing wrong with advertising or commercials, but many consumers still feel like any business owner using advertising is only trying to sell them something—as opposed to genuinely sharing knowledge or information in news stories.

In today's fast-moving and very-connected world, you can grow your reputation by creating a "presence" via media exposure. The business reason for this is much more important than just feeding the old ego: the bottom line to you and your business is that people buy from people they know and trust. That's why authenticity, sincerity, and expertise are so important to the process. It is also why professionals hire me, to help craft the believability and sincerity that will grow their presence via media coverage.

Media coverage simply gives the audience the information to find you. Certainly, once the audience knows who you are, you have to do the rest. It's the coverage, though, that provides you, the business owner, with the visibility that creates the credibility.

Credibility comes from third-party endorsement. Traditionally, the audience of news viewers feels that legitimate media coverage offers that third-party endorsement, and in a form that could not be paid for. Most people still receive their news via television, radio, newspapers, and magazine, so a coveted spot can launch a person's career or validate a new product. As a media insider, I'm not entirely convinced that media coverage is always synonymous with an endorsement, but what matters is that viewers and your customers feel that way.

We do know, though, that if people trust you are the best choice based on seeing you in the media, they'll seek you out to do business with you. That brings us back full circle to this fundamental question: why can't your company ever get media coverage for something besides a fire in the lobby? Even when it comes to your own unique trade publications, the media has to "buy" your story or it won't generate any attention.

Is there a magic set of buzzwords that the media will respond to? The answer is not found in buzzwords, but rather in the clock and the calendar. The key to successful media attention is actually fairly simple, but is also widely misunderstood by many publicity wannabes.

This is another key point so grab your highlighter again for this:

> *The ability to garner media coverage will depend on you being able to correctly answer this question: Why should the audience or the media care about my story?*

In journalism school this was called WIFM, which stands for "what's in it for me?" The "me" in question is the viewer, the reader, the listener. In other words, why is what you have to say important to anyone else? Media professionals—like reporters, editors, producers, and news directors—learn that they must consider any information from the perspective of the audience. This is exactly what you need to do, too.

The FAT Theory

In today's weight-obsessed society, let's use a different acronym for successfully getting you press coverage, and that is FAT! With a little forethought, creativity and basic writing skill you too can make your news FAT and grab a little bit of that media attention.

FAT stands for:

- **F**ocused
- **A**ttention-grabbing
- **T**imely

Let's get this party started!

Focused

Your press release should be tightly focused on **one** thing. Do not cram several pieces or tidbits of information into the press release, no matter how interesting you may find those things. Because those budget cuts have reduced the number of people working in the media, you need to be well-focused if you want anyone to pay attention. Why? Feeling pressured and not having enough time to meet the next deadline means that reporters and producers won't deal with someone who doesn't really know what they are doing. To a media person, if you are unfocused in your story approach, that will translate to you being an unfocused interviewee, a potentially disorganized guest who will be late for the broadcast and worst of all someone who will not be able to speak in good shorts bursts of useable information.

In fact, any decent story may have more than one interesting angle, but you must discipline yourself to propose only one angle at a time. You should picture yourself having a laser-sharp focus. This is not always easy to do, and seems almost counter-intuitive. You might think that if you suggest many good angles related to your potential story, the media will find your that story is even more interesting. You would be wrong though. It doesn't work that way. Ask yourself "what is the one thing that I most want have noticed?" and then ruthlessly keep your writing and your communication about that one point.

Let's walk through a few examples to illustrate how this can work for you:

Case Study #1:

As a part of your business growth strategy, you are upgrading the quality of your staff. You've been working at this for months now, and have lured two new employees away from your rival competitors. You want to get the word out within your industry and in your community. As luck would have it, this is exactly the kind of story that industry publications, business publications, and some local publications are likely to use. You immediately sit down to pen a press release with the names of both new employees, you add details about the background and experience of each person, and you even go so far as to include quotes from them about why they are happy to be joining your wonderful company. Good stuff and a publicity homerun, right? No! Here's why:

- Inclusion of both people with all the salient details makes the announcement too long. The press people may lose interest before they even finish reading it. I will not be telling tales out of school if I tell you that many media people have the attention span of a gnat, so you've got to be succinct.

- You actually have the opportunity to get media exposure twice and on two separate occasions, once about each new hire. If you allow a little bit of time in between you can be the recipient of two articles. But by virtue of lumping the hires together into one overly long document, you may not get any coverage at all.

- With only slight message tweaking and the separation of the announcements into two different messages, you double your chances of media coverage **and** you signal to your customers and your competitors that you are a company on the move. You seem to be hiring great people "right and left," so you are now a force to be reckoned with!

Case Study #2:

You've just landed a huge new customer or piece of business. Congratulations! This exciting news means, among other things, that you will be adding to your staff. So you send out an announcement right away trumpeting the news and explaining the fact that you will now be hiring some additional people. I'll bet you can see where this is going. For much the same reason as in the first case, you should send one announcement to the press about the new client and then after a short period of time send another one about your planned staff expansion. The reasons:

- You have a chance with the first message to really elaborate on the new client, show them some love, and discuss the new synergistic partnership. You can include plenty of detail about the client. This is the type of story that industry publications and trade magazine eat up with a spoon. And as a bonus, you also have a happy and flattered client because you sent him a copy of your announcement directly, regardless of whether the media uses it or not. Talk about win/win!

- The staff expansion news is even more exciting and has the potential to appeal to a completely different kind of mass media than your first announcement. Expansion and employment will play well in a broader section of media, and can be picked up by local radio, local television, local cable, daily newspapers, **and** the industry and trade publications.

- Combining the information into one announcement could cost you exposure in one or both of these opportunities.

Case Study #3:

Your charity fundraiser exceeded your expectations, so you've picked the chairperson for next year and have already started planning the next event. Everybody loves a good cause, right? You start making calls to the media to give them **all** of the good news about the money raised, the new chairman and the next event. What's wrong with this picture?

- This is actually the most challenging of our examples. Charitable work is wonderful, and your organization is to be commended. But non-profit organizations tend to swamp media outlets with stories that just aren't big enough to warrant mass media coverage. You have to focus long and hard on what you are trying to achieve with media coverage. In this case, I would recommend **one** release but only about **one** aspect of your story.

- You should craft an announcement that focuses on **why** the organization was raising funds. The story is not the fundraiser; the story is the value and importance of the work of the charity for which you so successfully raised money.

- The new chairperson and the next event are too far in the future to warrant much media exposure. Refrain from detailing the future plans until the next event is either imminent or successfully concluded.

This process of focusing will help you cull your story down into its most important and essential element. This focus will also prepare to you to respond succinctly in the event that the media does 'bite" on the story. If a reporter, producer, or writer wants to expand on the focus, or even take the story in a new direction, that is perfectly reasonable. But your tight focus in the beginning allows your audience (in this case the media) to really mull over the story, and it lets your story grow more organically.

Focus also means giving serious consideration to the best audience for this news of yours, and more serious consideration to who is really likely to cover it. Think back to our case studies: your story may be perfect for online or printed trade publications, but *The Wall Street Journal* isn't really going to bite on an announcement loaded with specific industry-only terminology or interest. A broader but even more compelling announcement must be crafted to reach the national media and even local mass media like local TV and newspapers. Focus on getting the biggest bang for your communication buck. Trade publications can be a perfectly effective vehicle in many cases, even if they are not as sexy as *USA Today*.

Use your focus to cut your publicity teeth. Successfully getting media coverage on a small or local scale leads to bigger and better publicity in the future.

One cautionary note about your newfound focus: by taking the Focus aspect of FAT to heart, you may now believe that you have two announcements. But check this theory with a few trusted colleagues. You may discover that only one piece of information really interests anyone. Sometimes the trees block our view of the forest so getting some extra and honest input may help you through the process.

We've bitten off the "F" in our FAT process of getting media coverage. Get ready to focus your attention on the Attention-Grabbing aspect:

Attention Grabbing

When you sit down to craft an announcement for the news media, it is vital that the headline be attention-grabbing, or else your announcement is on the fast track to the delete button. The headline is the headline! *Huh?*

> *Simply put, the headline will either make or break your story when it comes to grabbing attention.*

A good headline that can "hook" your audience is important in all professional communication. And you can find many articles and books about writing professional headlines, so feel free to knock yourself out with those tips if you really want to. But what I'm talking about here is slightly different.

The aforementioned books are all written for professional journalists or serious bloggers and are designed to give them tips on getting the masses to read the rest of their story, or to stay tuned for the rest of their story. You need to do a slightly different type of headline writing—because you are writing or "selling" this story to an audience of one person. When attempting to get publicity in the news media, you are only communicating with a single reporter, or one editor, or an individual producer. Of course, some of the basics of good headline writing do apply here, but since you have an audience of a single person it will be easier for you to find ways to be attention-grabbing, because you only have to get inside the mind of one person and not tens, hundreds, or thousands of people. Think of this is as your own personal Vulcan Mind Meld with the one person who can help get you publicity.

The primary job of the *headline* is to get attention. A good *headline* sells your audience into wanting to find out more by reading or hearing what comes next. As inspiration, let's use the thoughts of one of the greatest, most famous advertising executives that the modern world has ever known, David Ogilvy. He called attention getting headlines the "ticket on the meat." And Ogilvy explained that the headlines will flag prospective customers for the kind of product you are selling.

Here are the basic headlines about writing attention-grabbing headlines:

- Headlines should be short—less than two lines—and should very succinctly summarize the announcement
- You must force yourself to tell this "story" in one sentence
- Make the sentence an active, interesting statement
- Complete sentences are not necessary in writing headlines and can comfortably be avoided
- Unless you are making an announcement about a well-known celebrity, do not put a proper name in the headline

There is one final secret that many professional writers and PR folks frequently fail to use, and I will whisper that to you before the end of this chapter!

First, let's look at some examples. Here are some headlines I've recently written that were very successful in getting press and publicity attention:

Bubbles the Chimp will NOT inherit Jacko's Millions

Looking for Orlando's Youngest TV Reporter

Pink Slip Party Rides to the Rescue of Job Seekers

Here are some other good attention grabbing headlines:

Pianist keeps City's Singers in Good Tune

Jaycees Do Windows

It's Filing Frenzy Time and Tax Preparers Deduct Sanity

Can you tell what the successful headlines all have in common? Each headline is ten words or less. They are all written in an active voice. Like Ogilvy's meat metaphor, they all serve as the "flag" that compels you to pick up the "meat" of this story. Many are tied to some other real world **big** story, like tax time or unemployment. They are also clear, concise and interesting. It would have been easy to dull these down, and many people would have done just that. This is one of my favorite areas of expertise; I have loved writing headlines since journalism school. And now, with this book you will be able to write good headlines too.

On the other hand, here are the same headlines written in a fashion that is **not** attention-grabbing:

The Center for Great Apes Continues Fund Raising Efforts

Auditions Being Held

Carlos Gilder Announces Job Hunting Event to Be Held on Thursday

Local Piano Player Performs

Jaycees Help Homeowners

Tax Preparers Keep Busy This Time of Year

Sadly many press release and media announcement headlines fall into the latter category of uninspiring, uninteresting, and unsuccessful when it comes to getting attention from the media. Sad for the people trying to get some publicity, but good news for you, because you've just acquired a new tool to be much more successful in the attention-grabbing arena.

Our examples of successful attention grabbing headlines are cleverly written, but in your messages you also need to avoid these two things:

- being so cutesy that your audience will either groan or roll their eyes
- writing a headline that can mean something totally different than you intended

Of course, no headline-writing instruction would be complete without a few examples of unfortunate writing, and so here for your reading pleasure are some real "ripped from the news" headlines:

- **Chef Throws His Heart into Helping Feed Needy**
- **March Planned For Next August**
- **Police Begin Campaign to Run Down Jaywalkers**
- **Clinic Gives Poor Free Legal Help**
- **Farmer Bill Dies in House**
- **Workers Finish Boring Sewer Tunnel**

Remember that little headline writing secret that I promised you? It is simple tool to employ but not used often. That secret?

Write the Headline Last!

It seems almost counterintuitive, but for the novice it often works better than writing the headline before you craft the rest of your message. When you write your headline **last** you have already put together your press-worthy story, and you've kept it tightly focused on one thing. Nine times out of ten a well organized and focused message will practically write its own headline! Of course, some professional writers disagree with me and can't imagine writing without crafting the headline first. If it is important to you that you take a linear approach to writing, then by all means write your headline first. **But** be willing to return to your headline after you finish writing and see if you can create a new, snappier version to match your well-written announcement.

While there is an art to writing a truly great headline, most people can write a perfectly acceptable **and** attention-grabbing headline with a little bit of focused brain power.

Now it is time to tackle the last and most complex aspect of the FAT method of press and publicity:

Timely

Generally speaking, being *timely* means something is occurring at a suitable or opportune time. And the word *opportune* is perfectly suited to this section of the book. Publicity by definition is *opportunistic*, and trite as it sounds, timing is everything. America's favorite founding father Benjamin Franklin once observed, "You may delay, but time will not," and his words are perfectly appropriate when applied to timing press and publicity.

Creating a timely announcement means positioning your news announcement as relevant and current. Some business people find this difficult or counterintuitive, but as a media professional and publicist it is my favorite and a very rewarding part of this process. I will grant you that I am a true news "junkie" which makes getting publicity for my clients a much easier proposition. But it will become easier with practice. As a starting point you should consider what is going on around you locally, regionally, nationally, and industry-wise so that you can relate to your story. As examples:

Example #1

- Your story:
  Breaking ground on an addition to your warehouse

- Your timely story:
  Business expansion is great news for today's sagging local economy

Example #2

- Your story:
  Your charity is holding a Kid's Fun Day
- Your timely story:
  With childhood obesity on the rise, exercise for children is more important than ever

Example #3

- Your story:
  Starting your own new business
- Your timely story:
  Becoming an entrepreneur is the newest solution for would-be job seekers

Example #4

- Your story:
  You have just created a line of kid's vitamins
- Your timely story:
  With food prices increasing steeply, it can be difficult to get all the vitamins and minerals kids need each day without breaking the bank buying groceries

Example #5

- Your story:
  Your company landed a new account
- Your timely story:
  Your employees are demonstrating outside-the-box thinking in tough economic times

Example #6

- Your story:
  Your dental practice has added invisible braces

- Your timely story:
  With 1 in 10 Americans looking for a job, improving the smile could be the edge someone needs to succeed in the job market

Example #7

- Your story:
  You've just wrapped up a successful fundraiser for the Alzheimer's Foundation
- Your timely story:
  Because of the baby boomer population bubble, nearly 6000 Americans turn 65 every single day. Alzheimer's affects about 10 percent of people over 65.

The good news is that this is just the tip of the timely iceberg! These examples are all related to current socioeconomic factors occurring today. In addition to those current event types of opportunities, you can focus your timely messages around holidays, the school schedule, weather events, changes of season, etc.

But here is the key to being timely:

> *You should be prepared to act quickly and you must seize the day. The chance for being "TRULY TIMELY" is short.*

The perfect press and publicity opportunity may open suddenly and can snap shut just as quickly. So delivering timely messages to the news media is no small feat. When you solicit press and publicity, you are entering the arena of the news business. And make no mistake, regardless of whether you are contacting local or national media, radios or newspapers, magazines or television, there are rules of engagement.

> *"This time, like all times, is a very good one, if we but know what to do with it."*
>
> —Ralph Waldo Emerson

Ralph might well have been talking about timely press coverage! This is the most difficult aspect of the FAT method of publicity because it requires that you do all three steps correctly and simultaneously!

Act and React Quickly

What does acting quickly really mean? It means that in addition to planning for regular seasonal events, holidays and longer lasting socioeconomic trends, you should also plan for the things that you cannot anticipate because some big news and weather events will suddenly occur. When you are able to react and act quickly, you will be the publicity beneficiary.

Consider these examples of sudden unexpected events:

- oil spill in the Gulf of Mexico
- outbreak of a disease
- negative news about a public figure
- occurrence of a crime

All of these events bring specific publicity opportunities to my mind, and I have counseled a number of clients successfully through them. But how and why can you capitalize on things like this?

The Media Needs Good Stories

The reason you **should** be opportunistic and maximize these stories for your own benefit is because the media **needs** related news content. The media needs to supply context for a story, solutions to a problem, different angles for their own customers, and you can be the beneficiary. It can be challenging to find your perfect angle quickly, particularly as a media outsider. This is the time where good publicists really shine. However with some practice, you can develop this skill. Let's look at the categories of opportunity:

Oil spill in the Gulf of Mexico:

- resorts
- food industry
- law firms
- medical practices
- trade schools
- moving companies
- realtors
- environmental engineers
- non-profit organizations

Outbreak of a disease:

- manufacturers of safety gloves and masks
- medical practices
- continuing education
- health clinics for children or the elderly
- cell phone stores
- website/software developers
- pharmacies

Negative news about a public figure:

- mental health experts
- non-profit organizations
- law firms
- authors

Occurrence of a crime:

- home security
- hardware stores
- gun shops

- karate teachers
- dog trainers
- home remodelers
- realtors
- gated communities

Really sharp media people can find a way to make nearly any news story relate to a current and sudden, big story. It happens to be a skill that comes naturally to me, and I've been teaching it to media and non-media people for years. You only need to find a way to make a big story relate to your business, your specialty, your area of expertise. If your relationship to the story is tangential, the opportunity is for you to be quoted or on camera talking about the story as an "expert" in the field. You will **not** be talking about your own business; you are merely getting some initial exposure. If you do have a specific product, service, etc. that is related to the story, you can use this as the opportunity to discuss that.

The beauty of the FAT method of press and publicity is that it will work for you specifically because it will work for the news media.

Ask Not What the Media Can Do for You, Ask What You Can Do for the Media

Granted, that is a self-serving adaptation of the JFK quote, but apt nonetheless. If you understand how the media works and what they need and you offer that to them, you will begin to get press and publicity exposure.

FAT works because:

- your **FOCUS** will be noted and appreciated
- your **ATTENTION GRABBING** will do just that
- being **TIMELY** will position you to supply unique, fresh angles of context

How cool is that? You get what you need. The media gets what they need. Score!

According to Shell Horowitz, the owner of FrugalMarketing.com and co-author of *Guerrilla Marketing Goes Green*,

> *I've been featured in literally hundreds of newspaper and magazine stories, as well as radio segments, blogs, online magazines. My experience shows that media coverage doesn't always generate very much direct interest in my products and services—but it's tremendously influential as a credibility-builder. When people are considering buying something from you and they see you've been covered in the New York Times, Wall Street Journal, etc., it makes them pay attention.*

Couldn't have said it better myself.

When it comes to media attention FAT is where it's at!

If you've been paying close attention, you've noticed that I don't use the words "press release" much. The reason dear reader is simple:

Standard Press Releases Are Prehistoric

The standard press release has gone the way of the typewriter, carbon paper, white-out, rotary dial phones, and gas station attendants. Gone are the days of carefully crafted announcements on good quality paper, stuffed into envelopes or faxed to editors. Media people do not want more paper. They do not want long rambling cliché-ridden self-serving press releases. The standard press release has been replaced by a media alert that is sharply focused, gets right to the point and is relevant. Sounds a lot like the FAT theory, doesn't it?

This is the era of the **Media Alert** or the **News Announcement**. The FAT method definitely applies and should be used electronically and orally only.

In the age of the **Media Alert** and the **News Announcement**:

- The entire announcement should be in the body of an email
- Do not send attachments unless specifically requested
- The subject line is important
- Call the media with your media announcement or email it, but not both
- Have an electronic copy ready to send *after* a phone call
- Post your Media Announcement news on your company or personal website
- Search engines like Google will find your announcement if it exists online
- You may embed links if you reference a website, but do so judiciously
- You must ascertain the correct email address for sending

I recommend that you do **not** send faxes and you do **not** snail mail a press release. The reasons are simple:

- speed matters
- being perceived as contemporary and current is important
- media people are almost exclusively focused on computer and mobile devices when gathering news stories

Now you've finished digesting the FAT theory and you know that when you correctly seize an opportunistic media coverage moment, it will be good for you, and good for the news media, too. The old standard paper press release sent via snail mail or fax is outmoded, and will make you seem outmoded too.

Structuring your news story proposal correctly is only the first course in this evolving feast. Now that you have a great story idea you need to understand the next step and in the words of the unforgettable *Ghostbusters*, "who ya gonna call?

Chapter 3

Setting the Table:
Getting Media Appearances

- Where Does My Story Fit?
- Who Do I Contact?
- How Do I Get a Foot in the Door Without It Being Slammed in My Face?
- What Do I Do to Prepare for a TV Interview So I Don't Look Silly?
- Ten Things the Media Loves
- Ten Things the Media Hates
- Do I Need to Spend Big Bucks to Get TV Publicity?

"It's not what you look at that matters, it's what you see."

—Henry David Thoreau

Feeling pretty FAT and happy at this point? That's good news. But your success with the FAT method of publicity **also** requires that you get your Media Alert into the hands of the right people.

Where Does My Story Fit?

Before we detail who does what, we have to understand "what." Let's break the news-gathering process down. The mass media usually works on three kinds of stories each day:

- Breaking News
- Follow-up Stories
- Enterprise Reporting

Breaking News is also sometimes referred to as the Big News stories that were explained earlier. They are typically done as "same day" stories. That's pretty self-explanatory.

The news media will do **Follow-up Stories** to the Big News within 24 hours. Depending on the magnitude or gravity of the story, the follow-up reporting may even go on for 48 to 72 more hours. These Follow-up Stories offer background and clarity to help people understand how or why something has happened. Often the Follow-up Stories will also provide solutions for preventing this kind of problem in the future.

In the absence of Breaking News or needed Follow-up Stories, the media also does a third type of story called **Enterprise Reporting**. This Enterprise Reporting type of story is a news story that takes longer to investigate and research, involves more interviews, can be longer in length, and sometimes gets advertised or promoted in advance. Enterprise Reporting stories are written about topics that are not necessarily closely related to the Big or Breaking News stories, and can span several days. Enterprise Reporting stories include topics such as:

The Dirtiest Restaurant Kitchens

The Dangers of Wearing High Heeled Shoes

The 10 Best College Degrees

Most Livable Cities in America

Fun Family Trips on One Tank of Gas

The Purity of Bottled Water

Calorie Count of School Lunches

City Employees Goofing Off on the Job

What does all of this mean to your efforts to generate your own publicity? Simply that because your FAT opportunity will almost always occur in the Follow-up category and sometimes in the Enterprise category, you need to understand the different types of stories. If you grasp the timing of stories, it will be much easier to be timely with your own story.

Lest you be thinking that this is a simple process, you should also know that being timely means slightly things in different media. Timely in television and radio could happen as quickly as the very next newscast: only minutes or hours away. Timely in the print media means a story the next day or the next publication; and online news publications can use information almost instantaneously. One of the most important aspects of making yourself timely is that you are able to efficiently contact the correct person for each media outlet. Without knowledge of who you should speak with or email, you can waste valuable time, and your story will be outdated before you've even gotten in the door.

Who Do I Contact?

I spent a number of years on the inside of the media, so I can walk-the-walk and talk-the-talk with the rest of the media on my client's behalf. You, too, will need to fully know the media outlet you are approaching, understand the distribution method, and know their target audience. As a business person who wants to be taken seriously in the publicity arena, you must understand the skill set, expertise, or interest of the individual you are contacting. To start with, your first line of media contact can take shape like this:

In television you may contact:

- Assignment Editor
- News Director, Vice President of News, or President of News
- News Anchor, Show Host
- Producer
- Reporter

In radio you can contact:

- News Director
- Program Director
- On-air Personality

At a newspaper you can contact:

- Features Editor
- Assistant Editor
- News Editor
- Reporter
- Columnist

At a print magazine you can contact:

- Publisher
- Editor
- Reporter

In online magazines you can contact:

- Editor
- Writer

When you make the initial contact, you should speak professionally and listen closely. If you are contacting the wrong person, you may be on the receiving end of a nasty-gram email or a curt phone hang-up. Do not despair, just offer up a sincere apology and politely ask for the name of the correct contact. There are also services that supply all of the names and addresses, but those services are fairly pricey and designed for experienced users. A little time spent online researching your media target will typically yield you decent results without spending a pretty penny.

It is critically important that you have your ducks in a row, your story straight, your media pitch focused when you make your media contact. For the largest national media opportunities, you need to know several other contact secrets. Due to an enormous number of requests, submitting a story, topic, or guest to a national media outlet requires more digging to find the right entry point. When I secure national coverage for clients, I also take these extra steps:

- Research the company who produces the program (the television syndicate or the print publisher)
- Submit your info to multiple contact points simultaneously to ensure that you've gotten the attention of the right person
- Be willing to adjust your message to fit into the topics that are already on the published planning schedule
- Be flexible enough to bide your time until a reasonably good time and opportunity arise (trust me, they will)

So now you have a good idea of who to contact, based on where you think your story should appear. You are mindful of the suggestions about writing FAT media alerts. But there are a few additional reasons that some reporters will disregard your announcement. We need to spend a moment on the reporter-interviewee dynamic.

How Do I Get a Foot In The Door Without It Being Slammed in My Face?

Sometimes successful media coverage involves some psychology. You should consider the subtle signals you are sending in your press releases. The most obvious signal is in the way your press release looks. Not how it reads: how it looks. In Chapter 6 you will find specific examples of the correct way to set up an announcement, and it will matter to some reporters. And although it may seem trivial, this subtlety can land your info in the so-called circular file faster than you think.

Make sure that the page is set up the right way. Some reporters get hundreds of press releases every day with compelling stories. The reporter uses much discretion to pick and choose which ones he wants to follow up on. If you don't know enough about press and publicity to lay out the release correctly, the reporter is going to assume there's much more that you don't know. Until you take the time to learn the rules of the game, no reporter is going to waste his time coaching you through the process.

The second reason that your announcement won't make the news coverage cut is that you've sent it to the wrong person. This is an area is where having a publicity pro on your team can really help you. Roz Joseph, Global Media and Public Relations Consultant, shares a powerful learning experience of her own:

> *For years I have pitched assignment editors on different aspects of subject, trends and issues in the art market—attempting to impart information that would benefit collectors. Young to the PR field and media landscape I immediately targeted Assignment Editors, as I thought individual reporters would be swamped with requests and not have the time. Then I started really studying the writings of individual reporters, learning about their beat and sometimes picking up on their angst. I try to meet personally when I can and have conversations about the overall subject and industry. This means that I would have to*

conduct some research and educate myself on a variety of topics in the market. What's going on at auctions? Who's purchasing art at astronomical levels? What's going on in terms of fakes and frauds in the marketplace? What is provenance? How should collectors protect themselves? I am slowly building a reputation as the person to go to for expert opinion in the North American market.

The third reason some media alerts get trashed is they are too self-serving. You should be providing the reporter with so much great, interesting, reliable information that the reporter will look good to their own audience. Why does this matter? Back to that psychology! Self-serving media alerts will not be well-received or even used.

If you make the reporter look good by making his story interesting and exciting, he'll do a semi-sales job for you by himself and that will be far better received by the audience. When you share your great information the reporter seems to approve your message, which is actually a very strong endorsement from someone the readers or listeners trust. When you help people solve their problems, when you help a reporter solve people's problems, you won't have to pitch yourself and your business. It will be very clear that you have the answers people have been looking for. This is a win/win for the media and for you.

Make it clear to your media contact that you are the best person to do this interview. If possible cite a few of your relevant past works or experiences that make you a good interview option. Be confident but not cocky and explain that you have quality information that can then be passed on to the audience.

After you send a solid message to someone in the media, make sure that you leave your correct contact information. You'd be amazed at how many people don't do this correctly. Include a phone number and an email address that you check frequently.

You can also include additional press materials with your letter in order to avoid having your media contact do some extra research on your topic. Extra information that you can include in a secondary document would be:

- potential questions for you to be asked
- websites with backup information
- a brief summary of other recent stories and facts

Now you've crafted a smart announcement and gotten it in the hearts, heads and minds of the right people. Excellent work! Then the phone rings or your email inbox dings and you've gotten a response from someone in the media. Even better! You've gotten a foot in the door, and now you have to keep the door from being slammed on your fingers. The correct course of action for you now is:

ACTION!

Respond as quickly as you can! If you do **not** respond quickly the media will move on to another person that they can reach more quickly. Use the same communication mechanism as the person who contacted you. Reply via email to an email, return a phone call with a phone call. This is the outcome you've been working so hard to achieve so be upbeat and enthusiastic when warranted. As a media professional it is hard for me to admit this but the people in the media have super-sized egos. So this is not the time for you to have an outsized ego, or any ego at all for that matter.

What Do I Do to Prepare For a TV Interview So I Don't Look Silly?

Now you have the basic underpinning, you've got the attention of someone in the media and you are ready for your first interview. What? You've got cold feet? You are afraid that you will look nervous or silly? No worries, years of prepping people for live and taped interviews has given me a short list of little tricks that you can use.

Got that trusty highlighter handy? A quick note so that you don't approach this aspect too casually:

> *It is wonderful that you are a talented speaker, have a charming personality, and are a good conversationalist, but that does not necessarily make you media savvy . . . sometimes the opposite is true!*

If you're interested in successfully getting publicity you will need to focus on learning the mechanics of an interview and fundamentals like sound bites and message consolidation. Being interviewed is a completely different beast than being a delightful, charming person in real life! Watching, listening to, and reading other interviews are great places to begin. You should be able to respond to any question with short, concise, confident statements.

When you sit down for the interview, it is important that you appear as relaxed as you can. I don't believe in telling interviewees to "be yourself" because as "yourself" you are not accustomed to being interviewed. On the other hand, my years behind the camera coaching and cajoling nervous clients have taught me the following tips that will make you feel more comfortable during the interview:

1. Before the interview, you should rehearse your basic points **out loud** and then again out loud and in front of a mirror. Based on the questions you expect to be asked, also rehearse your answers **out loud** with **someone else** listening to you.

2. When you sit down for the interview, take a few deep breaths and then speak more slowly than you normally would. This holds true regardless of what type of media the interview is for, or whether it is live, taped, or on the phone. Speaking slowly gives you time to gather your thoughts, and will also make you seem intelligent and reasonable.

3. For in-person interviews, look the interviewer **in the eyes.**

4. If you don't know the answer to something, simply say that you don't have an answer but will be happy to find that answer after the interview. A good fallback response if you just need a moment longer to consider your answer is the ubiquitous, "That's a really good question . . ."

5. Be thoroughly versed on every aspect of the story, even the parts that don't pertain to you. Read up, go online, and watch television. Be as expert as you possibly can. Have facts, figures, and details at your fingertips and in your head.

Preparation = Success

The last tip about being completely up-to-speed on a topic is very, very important. Because you work in your own field, you probably know all or most of this information anyway, so it's merely a question of making sure you have the latest and greatest tidbits. Preparation will make your media exposure a home run.

Let's look at how this intensive prep will work for your ultimate success. Let's stick with two of our case studies from Chapter 1. We will look at how strong prep relates to a Breaking News Story interview and we will also look at the best way to participate in an Enterprise Reporting story.

Case Study #1:

The Breaking News Story: Occurrence of a Crime

Your publicity opportunity: You Own a Home Security Company

Your preparation means you should know these ten things before the interview, and have them committed to memory:

1. number of similar crimes that have occurred in the last week, month, and year
2. crime rate comparisons year to year
3. crime rate comparisons by geography—locally, regionally, nationally
4. most used solutions to preventing similar crimes
5. status of the victim
6. status of the perpetrator
7. any viable do-it-yourself solutions
8. your specific solution
9. how your solution compares price-wise to your competitors
10. things that may seem like solutions but are not

Will you be called upon to discuss all of this information? Probably not. Should you be knowledgeable and current about this information anyway? Absolutely, yes. Why?

- You will feel more confident because you will be more knowledgeable
- Being more confident will make you a better interviewee
- You may have the opportunity to work some of this information into the interview, and increase your own credibility as a trusted expert
- Your media contact will be impressed and make a mental note that you are a good source for this type of information

Case Study #2:

The Enterprise News Story: Unemployed People Are Having Plastic Surgery and Dental Procedures Even though They Have Very Little Money

Your publicity opportunity: Your Dental Practice Has Added Invisible Braces

Your preparation means you should know:

1. current percentage of unemployment locally, regionally, and nationally
2. year-to-year comparisons of unemployment figures
3. the average amount of time now being spent finding a job
4. types of people having most trouble finding employment (age, gender, ethnicity)
5. types of people having most success finding employment
6. career fields that offer the highest likelihood of finding a job
7. any costs associated with finding a job (wardrobe, resume, etc)
8. whether or not plastic surgery is increasing
9. whether or not cosmetic type dental work is increasing
10. the average cost of cosmetic dentistry

I can imagine that you might be feeling a little grumpy because it isn't your job to know all of this information. True enough. But look at it this way: it **is** your job to be this prepared **if** you want to be a first-class interview, **if** you plan to signal your depth of knowledge to increase your credibility, and **if** you want to get on the list of people the media will return to over and over for interviews. I tell my clients that becoming a first class interviewee trumps their grumpiness any day!

Let's be very clear, being thoroughly prepared does **not** mean preparing to sell your product or service during your interview. That would be advertising! But being thoroughly prepared DOES mean that when it comes to the topic of the interview **you** really know what you are talking about. You will appear to be an expert in this field, the media knows it, and consumers will know it. And eventually consumers become customers . . . your customers!

Ten Things the Media Loves

The psychology of publicity continues for one last go around because if you have hopes of appearing in the media on a repeat basis, it is important to understand the things that most media professionals like and dislike. I've been on both sides and take every bit of this into consideration for my own clients.

Ten Things the Media Loves:

1. Your media alert is short, sweet and to the point about your topic and about yourself. Be brief and stay on topic.

2. Stories that are about subjects that are timely/or can be "bridged to illustrate significant relationship" to the most recent events in the news.

3. Full contact information provided along with the best times to reach you so there is no playing phone tag.

4. Promptness in responding to a request for an interview and a speedy call back.

5. A subject that is truly unique—and believable.

6. A clever, fresh, unique angle on a story.

7. A right-on story pitch based on the needs of the editorial calendar—especially if you can **wait for a slow news day** like government holidays. If the government isn't making news because it is closed for the holiday, reporters are scrambling to find something to cover. Pitch even an average story on a day when the media is starving for news, and you're much more likely to get coverage.

8. Stories with good visuals. . .true for print or TV. Reporters tell stories with pictures. If the pictures aren't there, the reporters won't be either.
9. Stories with a sense of urgency and mass impact.
10. You show respect for the media profession by treating your media contact in a professional manner.

Ten Things the Media Hates

Unfortunately, *here in the real world* it doesn't take much for journalists to get annoyed at the people who pitch stories. If you are handling your own press and publicity it can be even easier to make mistakes when trying to get the word out about your events, products, features or services.

Here are ten things you must avoid:

1. You assume the media is there for your own self promotion.
2. You hound the media person incessantly with lengthy emails, or you leave lengthy phone messages.
3. Not responding to a call from the media.
4. Off-topic pitches and responses that are either incoherent or have rambling answers, or long press releases that have no point.
5. No contact information given for the media to reach you.
6. Pitches that are irrelevant to a particular media outlet (e.g., pitching women's fashion to a sports magazine).
7. Stories that are self-serving and have no greater impact.
8. Boring pitches that have absolutely no new hook or angle (e.g., press release with a headline about a new product blah, blah, blah), or the same story pitched over and over again with no new angle, when the pitch was already given a "no" because no means no.

9. Personal stories about people that are not well-known in situations that are not particularly unique.

10. Pitches made via social media.

It may seem by now that there is more work involved in this whole publicity effort than you thought. There is a bit of truth to that. I personally find it a lot of fun, but most of my clients tell me it is just plain old work! Regardless, it is the work that will best prepare you to be successful.

Do You Need To Spend a Ton of Money to Get TV Publicity?

Nope. You just have to be smart, creative and imaginative because obtaining press is as much about selling a good story as it is about writing one. Surprisingly, some sixty percent of the "news" found in the average newspaper was "placed" there by a PR person in some fashion. The publicist did this by convincing the media contact that the reading and viewing audience would want to have their information!

I'm not knocking professional public relations folks or publicists, many of them do a great job. Some of my best friends are publicists, and I'm very successful at it myself. On the other hand, it isn't brain surgery either, and if you are serious about doing it yourself then you can definitely make it happen. The reason that I only take on small number of clients at any given time is because getting press and publicity requires diligence and tenacity and observation. Just as a side note, here is a little primer about how good publicists approach media coverage:

A good press and publicity professional will:

- understand how to create a story with an angle that sells the story to the press
- already have media contacts who will take their calls

- understand editorial calendars so they can tailor stories to a publication's specific needs
- have the creativity and the instinct to "create news" by tying to topical trends or hard news events
- have the ability to turn up the jets when a big story arises

You do not have to spend a ton of money to get yourself on TV. But you do have to work at it and you do though have to play by the rules. Your effective use of press and publicity can be the perfect advertising for you. In the words of Mark Twain,

> *"Many a small thing has been made large by the right kind of advertising."*

Once you know who to contact it's time to make sure that your interview delivers everything you hoped, namely that you achieve your publicity goals as a part of a smart overall media strategy.

Chapter 4

Pull Up a Chair

- Review Your Business Goals
- Establish Your Publicity Goals
- Develop a Media Strategy
- Planning To Be Opportunistic
- Why Advertising Is Not the Evil Empire

"Vision without action is a daydream. Action without vision is a nightmare."

—Japanese proverb

We've spent three chapters discussing mass media and the best ways to get some valuable press and publicity for yourself and your business. Now let's focus on business, goals, and strategy. Publicity is good for the ego, we can admit that. For press and publicity to be truly effective though, it should be aligned with your personal or business goals. Your own self-satisfaction is all fine and good, but is secondary to the real value of publicity.

This is not intended to be a business book, and the assumption is that you have already developed specific business objectives that are aligned with your desire for publicity.

Review Your Business Goals

Let's spend just a minute with a quick review of SMART business objectives. A brand manager at Nabisco taught me the SMART approach years ago, I use it with my clients now and it bears a quick repeat:

The 5 Rules of Setting Objectives: Be SMART!

SMART represents the five characteristics of an efficient objective. It stands for:

Specific - **M**easurable - **A**ttainable - **R**elevant—**T**ime bound

Let's look at some examples that would be related to publicity.

Be SPECIFIC!

In this case, being "specific" means being "precise."

Example: "I need some publicity", doesn't work as a specific goal because you did not articulate with any specificity. It is unclear what the "some" means: it can be local publicity, national, TV, radio, trade publications, or any number of things. A much better objective would be "I need our ribbon-cutting ceremony to be covered by the local television station." In this case you and your team will know exactly what you expect and you will have a better chance of achieving success.

Be MEASURABLE!

When we say that an objective must be measurable it means you need to be able to measure, or track it. If an objective and the actions related to it are impossible to quantify, the objective should be reconsidered.

Example: "our press coverage must increase" is not a measurable objective. What exactly should we measure in order to find out if the objective was met? Increase from what and to what? If we change this to "our press coverage must increase from zero interviews to one interview per quarter," we've got a measurable objective.

Be ATTAINABLE!

Think this through and be honest with yourself: is it really possible to attain the publicity goals you've set or are you headed for disappointment? Set objectives that have a realistic chance of succeeding. Attainable is not necessarily "easily" achieved, so feel free to set "stretch goals" as long as they're realistic and not futile.

Example: you own a new real estate company and you set the objective of "becoming the best-known real estate company in the city." The problem is that you only have two newbie realtors while all your competitors have at least ten experienced, well-connected well-spoken realtors with media contacts. Your goal is not attainable; a more realistic one would be "personally cement a strong relationship with three new media contacts."

Be RELEVANT!

Oddly enough, since we've spent many pages on media relevance, the use here is somewhat different. When we say that a business objective should be "relevant" it actually means using the correct goal for a given individual or team: you need to think about whether someone can act on this objective or if it is either irrelevant or impossible for the job they perform. An example would be for setting media coverage goals for low-level, introverted, or even bombastic people in your organization who don't have the ability to speak publicly as your representative. You should craft objectives for the best people (including yourself) that you really want showcased and that the media will enjoy working with.

Be TIME BOUND!

This is probably the easiest to understand of the whole SMART goal setting process.

For example, if you just say, "We need to increase our name recognition," you will never be able to tell if the objective was achieved or not. Instead say, "We need to secure three radio interviews by March first." Now you can see if the goal was attained. Without a clear, distinct timeframe, no objective can succeed.

Ready, Set, Establish Your Publicity Goals

Okay, we've just finished our mini refresher course in setting high quality business objectives as they pertain to publicity. Now let's talk specifically about publicity goals. The first step in successfully planning publicity is establishing your intended goal.

An easy, effective and strategic way to define publicity goals is to start with a list of the reasons that you want publicity.

Here is a list of questions that I use with each new client and it is a good way to get you started:

1. Specifically what do you want to accomplish with publicity?
2. Who do you want to reach?
3. Based on their age, gender, and geography, what mass media does your target audience use?
4. What are all the ways to reach your audience?
5. What topics are they interested in?
6. Which local media can help (including college television, small radio stations, local cable news)?
7. Which statewide media can help?
8. Which national media can help?
9. What groups/businesses can help you?

10. How much time and how many resources do you have available to achieve this?

If you've decided that generating publicity about yourself, your products, or your business in general will help grow your brand or your sales, then answering this set of questions will help you set the right publicity goals. Just like with setting business goals, if you don't establish a road map for publicity you will never know if you've arrived at your destination!

Essentially, when you approach the business of media coverage you'll look at your goals for the publicity, who you want to reach with publicity, how you're going to reach that audience, and the best time to do so. It's also a good idea to decide how you will want to evaluate the success of your publicity.

Your publicity plan can be simple or elaborate depending on your specific goals, whether you want to alert local media to an upcoming event or generate a nationwide publicity campaign for your new product launch. You should also continue to watch the media analytically. Now that you understand how media really works, you should be able to ascertain where each story might have originated and which kind of stories seem to appeal to the media you're interested in. This is valuable information to apply to your own plan.

Be as specific as possible with your goals, because they'll guide the rest of the process. Next, establish your target audience. In broad strokes, these might be potential customers, potential employees, government officials, other businesses in your area, etc. Knowing who your audience is allows you to research their habits and make the best decisions about how to reach your target audience. The nice thing about mass media is that it IS mass media. In other words, it reaches many people simultaneously in a shotgun approach. So you will also reach many people outside of your target audience, but there is nothing wrong with that.

When you are working on getting media coverage you should continually circle back to your primary publicity message. What is your objective and what is the message or information that you really want to communicate? These won't necessarily be the direct subject of your press coverage, but should always be in the back of your mind. One tool I employ for my clients is the post-interview critique. We record or save the interview and then review it together. This is a great way to get a second opinion and a also a great way to determine if the interview went as well as it seemed to in real time. The post-interview critique leads us nicely to the evaluation stage of this process.

Evaluation

Even after you score the interview, blurb in the paper, or news story, don't forget to analyze how well the publicity worked after the fact. You should do an objective analysis so that you can be even better the next time. Internal satisfaction is a great thing, but external rewards are a much more strategic opportunity. Anecdotal responses, like hearing from your neighbor or the convenience store clerk that they saw you "on the TV" will make you feel good, but it doesn't give you much real information. Instead, consider evaluating it this way:

- How many media alerts did you send out?
- How many calls or emails did you receive from people who read your media alerts?
- How many calls or emails turned into stories, interviews, and mentions?
- How much interest did those stories generate for the business?
- Did you achieve the original publicity goal?

Lots of people set meaningless publicity goals, and then wonder why they don't see any business growth. Remember that the purpose of publicity goal setting is to move forward strategically. The publicity goal should be aligned with a business goal.

Publicity goal setting is a process, just like all goal setting. Evaluation is an important part of that process. So think about what you did, how you did it, and what you got out of it. There's always something to be learned regardless of the outcome; you discover what works or doesn't work for you, what works for the media and even *God forbid* why you failed. Understanding the process will increase your publicity success even more as you apply it consistently in the future. You also have to realize that achievement of a publicity goal is usually not an overnight process. You are going to have to work regularly at transforming your press desires into publicity goals and then achieving the goals.

Developing a Media Strategy

There is a big difference between publicity goals and a media strategy. Sometimes goals are described as "a dream with a deadline!" Many people know that they want press coverage but they have trouble creating a plan to get there.

> *Goals without action plans are just words.*

A media strategy is the specific route you plan to take in order to achieve your publicity goals. Strategy is really the mechanics of planning. Brand awareness, reputation and your bottom line can all affected by media coverage. So how can you devise a media strategy?

The word "strategy" tends to cause mental panic and a flurry of meetings. It doesn't have to be a painful process. A media strategy is simply a plan. A concise plan. It's a tool to help you focus your publicity and press coverage efforts. What can you do in a world where press coverage has the power to make or break you?

- Choose a media strategy that sets you apart. The best strategy is one that will separate your business apart from its competitors. There's no magic formula for such a strategy, but there are key factors that will help you determine what your strategy should be. You need to know exactly who your customers or target prospects are, where they are located, what they want and need, and why, how, and when they need it. And you need to understand how your competitors are being covered by the media. You don't want nor need to have the same message as your competitors because the basis for your coverage is as unique as you are.

- Keep your eye on the big picture. It's easy to get too wrapped up in day-to-day problems to see media opportunities when they do arise. That is precisely why people hire someone like me. If you are going to do this yourself, you need enough distance and perspective to see opportunity approaching while there's still time to do something about it.

- Locate or develop systems for dealing with the media. Who is currently responsible for working with the press in your company? Is it you? How was this person trained to deal with media enquiries? Has this person had any professional media coaching? How versed is this person in your company? How well-spoken, articulate, and camera-friendly is this person?

- Contact other people to find out how they handle media attention.

- Keep in touch with opinion makers in the community. Find out how you and your company are perceived in their eyes prior to your publicity efforts.

- Predict and plan. The more planning you get done in advance, the more effective your media work will be.

Work through these planning questions, keeping your answers as simple and clear as you can:

1. What are your communication strengths?
2. What are the major opportunities for communication with the media?
3. What are the major communication obstacles?
4. Have you developed the idea of how you would like to appear in the public eye?
5. What activities would you particularly like the public to associate with you?
6. Can you easily explain the aim of your media work? No journalist or potential customer will be able to understand it if you don't.
7. Do you need to find potential case studies before you start calling your media targets?
8. Do you need to collect photos or other examples, or even props, to illustrate your stories?
9. Is there a negative way the media could present you or your event? Think through the ramifications and possible avoidance tactics.

A proactive strategy is designed to make the media work for you, using it to raise the company profile and keep potential customers aware of your expertise. As your knowledge of the media increases and as you acquire new learning, be sure to keep feeding that valuable information back into your media strategy. You'll need to keep revisiting your strategy.

After you are comfortable that you have worked through the necessary background . . . drum roll please . . . you are ready to develop your own strategic, goal-aligned, press and publicity plan!

As you start this phase, you can create additional synergy by arranging to have your public relations plan coincide with other marketing and sales efforts. Decide what communication vehicles you will use to get your message to the public via the media. Examples would include:

- press conferences, interviews, or media tours
- radio, television, or press interviews
- seminars or speaking engagements
- event sponsorships
- media alerts
- articles
- customer success stories
- letters to the editor

Clearly, you cannot control the interview portion of this plan, since the media either bites on a story or not. But you should still decide what items on this list will be your focus. And one nice benefit of this list is that so many things go hand-in-hand. You can send a media alert to announce a seminar. You can use a press conference to explain an event sponsorship. You can use an event sponsorship to disseminate your articles. You can do another media alert to announce the reaction to your letter to the editor. And so on and so on and so on.

Planning To Be Opportunistic

Even with all of your smart planning and goal development it is critical that you remember:

> *Your press and PR plan has got to include information*
> *that is legitimate, relevant, interesting, timely and real.*

Do you recall that term from the old cowboy movies? After a really unpleasant experience the ranch hands were "snake bit." The media gets "snake bit" too. A reporter may use a quasi-story from you once, but they won't do so a second time and your efforts in the future are going to be exponentially more difficult.

*"If you are writing about baloney, don't try to make it
Cornish hen, because that is the worst kind of baloney there
is. Just make it darned good baloney."*

—Leo Burnett

This thought from advertising genius Leo Burnett serves as a good transition from press and publicity to advertising. Unlike some of my contemporaries I do NOT believe that advertising is a dirty word.

Advertising Is Not the Evil Empire

There is room in a good media strategy for both publicity and advertising and they can often complement each other very nicely. I will detail some specifics for you, but the headline is that the difference in advertising is that YOU can control the message. No psychology here! In an interview you have very limited control over the message, but that model changes completely with advertising. How?

- Advertising can not only explain the features and benefits of a product, but also provide information that helps consumers make an informed buying decision. If you have developed a product or service that you feel is better than anything currently on the market, advertising allows you to unabashedly tell the world.
- Advertising can demonstrate specific features and benefits and introduce special promotions or pricing. You can show how your product or service works and how it's packaged so prospective customers will know what to look for at the point of sale.

- Advertising clearly conveys your business name, the type of products or services you offer, and the days and hours you are open.
- With advertising frequency, you can keep your name in front of consumers. If your customers see a commercial dozens of times, the next time they need that product they will be likely to buy the one they remember.
- Advertising is so powerful that if a business stops advertising, it may give the impression that they've gone out of business. When people see a business advertise for a long period of time and then stop, they may get the false impression that the business is no longer open, even though they are! That's powerful stuff.

Advertising is defined as a form of communication intended to persuade an audience (viewers, readers or listeners) to purchase or take some action about products, or services. Advertisements typically include:

- the specific name and location of a product or service
- exactly how that product or service could benefit the consumer
- persuasion of the target market to purchase or to consume that particular brand

Advertising is designed to **sell**. Of course, unlike press and publicity you do have to **purchase** advertising. But there is a reason that it has been in existence since the beginning of time! Did you know that the Egyptians used papyrus to make sales messages and wall posters? And that commercial messages and political campaign displays have been found in the ruins of Pompeii and ancient Arabia? And the reason is? Because advertising works!

According to Sharon DeLuca, President of SDL Communications, Inc., the advantages of paid advertising over unpaid press and publicity are numerous:

- Control of the creative message. Free news coverage of your product or service is sometimes presented incorrectly by the media.

- When purchasing media, you research consumers' spending and buying habits through demographic and qualitative profiles, then target your media purchase to best reach your potential client efficiently and effectively.

- Advertising in certain media such as news shows, endorsements by personalities and consumer publications are often thought to be as credible as interviews in those same programs and publications.

Some ad campaigns have been so well known and successful that they've become a part of our shared media history. Remember these oldies but goodies?

- Nothin' Says Lovin' Like Something from the Oven— Pillsbury
- We're Number Two: We Try Harder—Avis
- When It Absolutely Positively Has to Be There Overnight—Federal Express
- We Make Money the Old Fashioned Way: We Earn It— Smith Barney
- Finger Lickin' Good—Kentucky Fried Chicken
- Where's the Beef?—Wendy's
- Snap, Crackle, Pop—Rice Krispies
- Just Do It—Nike

Publicity and paid advertising can feed off of each other: in 2006 a major overseas ad agency created a **paid advertising campaign that actually got tons of media coverage by NOT appearing on the air.** The particular campaign was devised for Tourism Australia and was summarily rejected by the broadcasting powers in the United Kingdom. The Aussie ad campaign asked the question, "So where the bloody hell are you?" and was deemed too profane for broadcast. (Note to self, the word "bloody" apparently plays a lot differently on the other side of the pond!) At any rate, the English viewing public was so intrigued by the fact that they could not see the commercials that the ad campaign began to gain traction even before it eventually made its way to the airwaves.

So the bottom line is that when advertising is used in tandem with your ability to generate publicity, it will make your message even more powerful. Keep in mind that advertising can also be an effective part of the media coverage and publicity mix.

You have identified the strategic media and publicity goals to achieve your business goals. You have taken a very smart well-thought out approach to publicity. All good news! Now it's time to switch from the left side of your brain which processes information in a linear manner and use the more creative right side to be a little more imaginative and a little less logical.

Chapter 5

The First Bite:
Your Best Shot at Actually
Getting Media Exposure

- ICCK Is Better than It Sounds
- Imagination
- Creativity
- Curiosity
- Knowledge

*"Think left and think right and think low and think high.
Oh, the thinks you can think up if only you try!"*

—Dr. Seuss

At this point, you've learned my FAT (Focused, Attention-grab-bing, Timely) method of getting media attention, you are thor-oughly schooled in setting SMART (Specific, Measureable, Achievable, Results-oriented, Time-bound) press and publicity goals…and so you may be feeling a little over-acronymed. But if you will allow me one final bowl of alphabet soup it will tie everything into a nice tasty package for you.

The ICCK Factor

Now that you have a goal, a plan and a topic it's time to craft an actual "pitch" for the media. This is where the rubber really meets the road; so get your highlighter ready again because:

> *Writing a successful message for the media requires that you suspend reality*

The key to getting the media to give your message a second glance is to wow them with your **ICCK** factor. In this approach, ICCK stands for **I**magination, **C**reativity, **C**uriosity, and **K**nowledge. Unless you are actively engaged in a creative endeavor regularly, this can be somewhat challenging.

Imagination

The very fact that you have decided to take advantage of this opportunity and position yourself via media alerts tells me that you are an imaginative sort. You should feel good about the fact that you can imagine or envision your publicity success and are already taking the steps to make it happen. Not everyone can employ their imagination so effectively and you already have a leg up on your competitors.

Creativity

Creativity comes much easier to some of us than to others. I've been known as a "creative type" my entire adult life and flattering as that may sound, it is also something that I've worked at developing and honing. Even during my years in senior management when I was no longer writing news copy or producing television shows and television commercials, I would employ as much creativity as possible in problem solving and brainstorming. As a publicist, I find that creative skills and creative problem solving bode well for my clients.

What's that you are thinking? You just aren't that creative? Not to worry, with practice the process can become easier. At the very least practicing creativity regularly means that your brain won't hurt as badly when you do need to apply it!

> *"A fool-proof method for sculpting an elephant: first, get a huge block of marble; then you chip away everything that doesn't look like an elephant."*
>
> —Author Unknown

Some people think that creativity has a limited application. If you are going to apply the ICCK tips you need to stop thinking that painters, writers, poets and the people in "creative fields" are the only creative people. Creativity can and does spill over to many fields and disciplines. It's not restricted to certain careers or occupations. It's about creative effort.

I've compiled a list of my favorite tips, these are things that I use and that other "creative types" rely on too. They should help put you in the right frame of mind for using creativity to pitch your story. I find that the first ten are the most powerful, but you may also find that the rest of the list contains exactly the impetus you need.

To develop a creative angle to use in pitching your story to the media:

- Stop telling yourself you're not creative.
- Creativity is a muscle. Exercise it daily.
- Consume information by the bucket load. The more you know, the more you can create from that knowledge.
- Let your mind wander. A wandering mind may allow your brain to search more widely for connections that could trigger a "eureka" moment.
- Seek out creative company. The best ideas are forged not in moments of solitary genius, but during exchanges with trusted colleagues.
- Get away from the computer. Take pen and notebook, and go somewhere new.

- Write down a list of ideas and draw random arrows between them.
- Generate a boatload of ideas.
- Avoid multi-tasking. It is impossible to get immersed in an activity if you are not totally focused on it.
- Don't try for perfect. Just get the ideas out there, as soon as possible and get feedback.

"Creativity is a lot like looking at the world through a kaleidoscope. You look at a set of elements, the same ones everyone else sees, but then reassemble those floating bits and pieces into an enticing new possibility"

—Author unknown

If you still aren't feeling motivated, energized and positive about your creative abilities, relax and keep reading:

- Stop visualizing catastrophes, and focus on positive outcomes.
- Listen to new music. Try something instrumental and rhythmic that you've never heard before.
- Recall your creative triumphs. It means you can create something equally wonderful again. In fact you can go out and create it today.
- Count your blessings. As well as feeling happier, it will inevitably help you be more creative too.
- Identify a compelling motive. You need a reason to be creative.
- Explain what you're really trying to say to an inanimate object.
- Consider it a worthy challenge. If a task is too easy, you don't need to be particularly creative, so your creative self will simply say, "You can manage this one without me."

- Provide a conducive environment. The optimal environment varies from person to person, so you'll need to experiment to find what works best for you.
- Allocate a committed block of time.
- Clean up your working space. Even if you are not a cleaning addict, a tidy desk helps to create a fresh start.
- Flip through a book containing thought-provoking images.
- Be open. Never shut down or judge any idea that comes your way.
- Think on paper. With a bunch of loose paper, start jotting ideas down.
- A change in surroundings can recharge your brain.
- Volunteer. Getting your hands dirty for a good cause can be the source of more inspiration than you'd ever imagine.
- Embrace your inner grouch. Discontent may just be a vast, untapped source of creativity.
- Cataloging your ideas is productive because it allows you to go back and take a second gander while viewing your ideas on much larger scale.
- Enjoy not knowing. Isn't it nice to have one small corner of your life where you don't know what you're going to do, or what's going to happen?
- Avoid logical thinking. It's often the enemy of truly innovative thoughts.
- Stop being practical. Practicality stifles innovative ideas before they can properly blossom.
- Allow your mind to be at play. You've heard the expression "work hard and play hard." They're the same thing to a creative thinker.
- Practice thinking. Think about things and formulate some opinions. They may be right, they may be wrong, but they'll be interesting.
- Surround yourself with creative people often.

- Don't choose the company of doubters and negative people. They will just pull you down.
- Do challenge conventions and the norm. Challenge everything.
- Do realize and remember that all creative people feel the same frustration and uncertainty as you do and some of the most successful are driven forward by tremendous self doubt. Turn the negative feelings into positive self-motivation.
- Immerse yourself in the task at hand. Do your research, read everything you can about your subject, attend seminars, ask experts for their input, and so on.
- Surround yourself with inspirational props, whether it's books on creativity, images you find inspiring, or creativity quotes.
- Identify your creative times. Choose those times when you know you will be the most creative.
- Don't force it. Stop. Do something else. When you get back you will feel far more refreshed and ready to get started.
- Right before you go to sleep, assign your brain the creative problem and tell it to find a solution. You will be amazed at how often it works.
- Criticize later, or some part of your mind may feel threatened and shut up and withdraw.
- Collaborate with new people.
- Try and find the pattern between things, and connect the dots between random things just for fun.
- Practice asking yourself how to do something differently.
- Be curious about everything.
- Write all ideas down immediately.
- Read wildly different things. Especially stuff you disagree with.
- Do it when you're excited.

- Don't be afraid to be stupid and silly. To be creative you must lose your fear of being wrong.

And finally:

- Stop reading creativity advice.

Why? Because in the words of a certain athletic company, "just do it." Experts who have studied the creative process sometimes compare creativity to courage, so "just do it" is an apt way to finish the list and get your creativity started all at the same time.

Read these terrific examples of ICCK creativity to keep those creative juices flowing:

You started an online dating service? Your media alert can start like this:

> *"I CAN FIND ANYONE THE LOVE OF THEIR LIFE IN 90 DAYS OR LESS!"*

Your accounting firm needs more clients? You produce a release with the headline:

> *"FINANCIAL WORRIES CAUSE MOST DOMESTIC VIO-LENCE"*

You started up a new hair-styling salon?" You sent a media alert to the media with the headline:

> *"HOW SHAMPOO KILLS HAIR!"*

I can tell you are already feeling super creative, so let's move on the next step.

Curiosity

Why is curiosity so important to the process of creating strong successful media alerts?

Curious people ask questions and mentally search for answers. The mental exercise caused by curiosity makes you better able to think outside of the box. When you are curious about something, your mind expects and anticipates new ideas. Just think, how many great ideas may have been lost due to lack of curiosity?

By being curious you will be able to see new possibilities which are invisible to other people. It takes a curious mind to look beneath the surface and discover new possibilities. So:

- Keep an open mind. Be open to learn, unlearn, and relearn.
- Don't take things for granted. Try to dig deeper beneath the surface of what is around you.
- Ask questions relentlessly. What, why, when, who, where, and how are the best friends of curious people.
- Read diverse kinds of material. Try to pick a book or magazine on a new subject and let it feed your mind with the excitement of new ways to look at things.

The more you question things, especially things in the news, the more ideas you will have about how to approach the media. Why do some people swear by global warming and others discount it completely? What causes the unemployment rate to shift so much from month to month? Who are the local movers and shakers? How did those people become the local movers and shakers?

Depending on your viewpoint, I happen to be either blessed or cursed with a very curious mind. Many good journalists have a curiosity about them too. My insatiable curiosity and my inquiring mind have helped unearth publicity approaches for my clients time and time again. There are two important reasons that curiosity is vital in our press coverage scenario:

1. The more informed you are about stories, opinions, and happenings, the smarter you can make your media coverage pitch
2. When you exercise curiosity, you will discover even more options for media coverage

This brings us to our final component for writing successful media alerts. And that is knowledge. Simply having a keen awareness and understanding of your business, other businesses, and the world around you won't just make you sound smarter; it will make you *be* smarter.

Knowledge

As Henry Ford put it,

> *"You must know all there is to know in your particular field and keep on the alert for new knowledge. The least difference in knowledge between you and another man may spell his success and your failure."*

I couldn't have put it any better myself, and it is absolutely on target when it comes to media alert writing. As we mentioned in Chapter 2 and in Chapter 3 it is important, at least while you are contemplating press and publicity, that you stay as current as possible about your own business and things going on around town and around the world. You may or may not be a person who regularly watches television news, reads newspapers, or gets news online. But it is absolutely worth your while to devote yourself to this task when it comes to media alerts.

Let's return to some of our earlier case studies and make them suitably ICCK.

- **Your story:** Breaking ground on an addition to your warehouse.
- **Your timely story:** Business expansion is great news for today's sagging local economy.
- **Your ICCK story pitch**: Unemployment just hit 12% in metro Orlando, and experts say it's even higher in the construction business. One local business plans to put some construction workers back on the job and chop away at high unemployment all at the same time.

- **Your story:** Your charity is holding a Kid's Fun Day.
- **Your timely story**: With childhood obesity on the rise, exercise for children is more important than ever.
- **Your ICCK story pitch:** What do the governor of Massachusetts, the head of the US Agriculture Department, Michelle Obama, and Major League Baseball all have in common? This month they have all joined the fight against childhood obesity! But you don't have to travel to Boston or the ballpark to teach your kids about healthy weight, you can do it right here in Tampa on Saturday at the Second Annual Kid's Fun Day.
- **Your story:** Your company landed a new account.
- **Your timely story:** Your employees are demonstrating outside-the-box thinking in tough economic times.
- **Your ICCK story pitch:** Motivational speaker Tony Robbins just debuted a new television show with a powerful message: "People who have reached the pinnacle of success in life do not sit on their laurels once they've reached the top. They keep striving for more." The employees at XYZZ Company live that motto every single day. And the proof is in their pudding! A team so strong that they put Donald Trump's *Apprentice* to shame has used powerful motivation and creativity to create a big new business success.

So when you are looking for press and publicity and you need to write the perfect media alert, remember to turn up the right side of your brain and be ICCK. Who knew that making something sound as undesirable as the word ICCK could be so effective?

Now you've come up with some interesting and exciting new publicity concepts, you are probably hungry to start sampling the world of publicity. Before you dive into the news coverage buffet, let's take a look at some examples that have gotten the media tongues wagging.

Chapter 6

Sampler Platter

- Sample Media Alerts
- Sample Story Pitch
- Sample Interview Prep and Questions
- Sample Interview Follow-up

"A pint of example is worth a gallon of advice."

—Author Unknown

It is difficult to get FAT if you don't sample anything! So learning the FAT method of press and publicity wouldn't be complete without some examples of successful methods. Here is a FAT sampler platter of media alerts, story pitches, interview prep questions and interview follow-up.

Sample Media Alerts

Let's start off with a media alert about an upcoming event for job seekers. Getting press coverage of an event can be challenging unless the event is positioned as being particularly timely. In the case of the **Pink Slip Party** we were able to capitalize on two timely opportunities: newly released unemployment numbers and the phenomenon known as speed dating.

For more info:

Contact:
Phone/fax number:
Email address:

FOR IMMEDIATE RELEASE

Orlando Unemployment Nears 11%
Pink Slip Party to the Rescue

The so-called Pink Slip Party combines the concept of speed dating with the exposure of a job fair. "A resume in one hand and a drink in the other" describes this hot new trend, and Orlando is soon to be home to a second Pink Slip Party.

Orlando FL, July 31, 2009 — For job seekers, recruiters, and even people just wanting to network, a Pink Slip Party is the perfect event. Unemployment in Central Florida is now higher than in the state of Florida overall, and also higher than the national average. Carlos Gill and his Pink Slip Party plan to change all of that!

Slated for August 19, the free event will run from 4 to 8 pm at Blue Martini at The Mall at Millennia. The event will be hosted by Carlos Gill's **JobsDirectUSA.com** and by **Jux-ta-pose.** Both party hosts are online job boards founded by "formerly pink slipped" entrepreneurs. And for the first time, the Pink Slip Party is co-sponsored by the nationally syndicated morning television news show *The Daily Buzz*.

At the Pink Slip Party, hopeful job seekers are given pink wristbands and recruiters are given blue wristbands to identify each other. Job seekers load up on resumes and network their way to their next job over cocktails. Gill comments, "If you need a job, need to hire, or simply want to network with hundreds of local professionals and have fun in a casual, relaxed environment, this party is for you. This is not your typical job fair; in fact it's far from it."

The Orlando-based *Daily Buzz* will be on hand to record all the action, and to give national exposure to this hot new concept. According to Buzz GM Sandra Gehring, "the real silver lining of this poor economy is the creativity of people like Carlos. And since online job applications and e- resumes are par for the course today…Pink Slip Parties really help put a face on good candidates and great companies."

Over 400 job seekers and recruiters turned out for Orlando's first pink slip party in June. Local recruiter Greg Inguagiato from Palm Coast Data says that after attending the first Pink Slip Party he "was so impressed by the caliber of job seekers, employers, and recruiters in attendance" that he vowed never to miss Gill's Pink Slip Parties.

Since early 2009, JobsDirectUSA.com, Gill's Jacksonville-based online job board, has put a new spin on the traditional job fair and has hosted over a dozen pink slip parties throughout Florida. The Blue Martini is a larger venue than the first Orlando pink Slip Party to hold an even greater turnout—which means more recruiters, and jobs.

- 0 -

You should note that good media alerts have a compelling, large, and bold faced headline. They also have a first paragraph in a smaller face but bold type, which succinctly summarizes the media alert.

Our next sample features the launch of what would become an ongoing commercial enterprise. The launch was a difficult concept to communicate briefly and clearly. The sample below includes a short quote from one of the company principals to make the media alert sound more personable. The timing of this release was also a consideration. Because holidays can be slow news days and the media is looking for good Enterprise Reporting stories, the release was sent out just prior to New Years Day.

FOR IMMEDIATE RELEASE

Seminole School Faculty Can Kiss their Stress Goodbye!

One of the tremendous benefits of exercise is stress reduction. But finding the time, the place, and the money to exercise can be difficult, especially if you work the long hours of school employees. Now there is a healthy twist on "Happy Hour" to the rescue.

Lake Mary, FL December 28, 2009 — The educators of today are the most important people that students will ever meet. That weighty responsibility means long, early hours for school employees—hours that make it tough to take care of their own fitness.

To recognize and thank the faculty, administrators, and staff who work in Seminole County, one local gym and personal training

---

studio is excited to offer a new **Happy Hour Teacher's Appreciation Program**. Designed especially to suit the schedules of school employees, Pro Fitness will offer this incredible and healthy educator opportunity.

Every Monday, Wednesday, and Friday, all SCPS employees and Seminole County private school employees can use the personal training studio and private gym for just one dollar ($1) a day from 3 to 6 pm.

"Too often we forget to say 'thank you' to our educators for their commitment, caring, and devotion to educating our young leaders of tomorrow," says Brooks Stogsdill of Pro Fitness. "We want to reward our educators the best way we know how, which is with our all new Happy Hour Teachers' Appreciation Program."

Happy Hour Fitness rewards educators with personal training, group fitness, and a fitness membership! The new Pro Fitness facility in Lake Mary/Longwood is centrally located, and so is ideally suited for teacher stress reduction. Any school employee with four quarters to spare has a new place they can call their fitness home! Pro Fitness is teaching the teachers to take Happy Hour to whole new healthy level.

For more info:

Contact:
Phone/fax number:
Email address:

- 0 -

As you know by now, timing is critical in securing press and publicity. The nonprofit organization in the next media alert created a fundraising opportunity because of the news events happening at the time. This is a good example of understanding that an event or activity may need to be created specifically to earn you some press and publicity exposure.

How do you spell O- P- P- O- R- T- U- N- I- S- T- I- C? This is a great example of being both opportunistic and altruistic. I would draw your attention to the use of a website in the body of the announcement. In the original version, this was an active hyperlink that let the reporters go to the website, check out the site and start formulating their own questions. The other noteworthy aspect is that a photo was included, because the subject matter lent itself to a cute irresistible image.

FOR IMMEDIATE RELEASE:

(Photo attached)

BUBBLES THE CHIMP WILL NOT INHERIT JACKO'S MILLIONS

Michael Jackson was well known for many things including as a high profile animal lover. But all rumors to the contrary, the singer didn't leave any of his rumored millions to his beloved chimp Bubbles after all. So Bubbles is now the new face of a much-needed fundraising effort.

Wauchula FL, July 25 — A tabloid headline could read, "No Jacko Bucks for Bubbles." Although he is definitely not a beneficiary named in Michael Jackson's will, Bubbles the chimp now leads a healthy, happy life. No more moonwalking and music video performances, the famous Bubbles is just one of twenty-eight chimps and fourteen orangutans housed at an ape-centered sanctuary in the rural quiet of central Florida.

It costs money to house, feed, and care for Bubbles though. Described on the website as smart, distinctive, and tender, Bubbles and his ape friends need financial help. So a new fund-raising campaign called the **Bubbles and Friends Fund** can be accessed at www.centerforgreatapes.com. Although Bubbles seems happy with the last four years of obscurity, his famous image is being employed now to help demonstrate that the Center for Great Apes and Bubbles himself do need donor support to survive.

The Center for Great Apes is a haven for ex-Hollywood simians frequently featured in movies, TV shows, and commercials—a retirement home for entertainment apes. The Center was a perfect spot for Bubbles who was sent there by his trainer Bob Dunn in 2005: a serene, natural habitat, away from the prying public eye.

Bubbles was adorable and cuddly as an infant, which is exactly why many chimps are used in commercials and on the silver screen. But like all simians, Bubbles became too strong and large to be controlled by Jackson or the animal trainers, so he "retired" from the entertainment biz at the ripe old age of six.

Although the Jackson family has always known Bubbles whereabouts, no monetary support for Bubbles has ever made its way to the sanctuary. And after a record eighty media requests this month regarding Bubbles, necessity and opportunity have converged at the Center for Great Apes.

Chimps like Bubbles live to be nearly fifty years old, so apes need forty-plus years of care long after they've passed the cute stage. According to Ragan, founder and director of the Center for Great Apes, "it takes $15,000 a year to care for even one ape, and like most non-profits we've begun to feel the economic pinch. And so a donation seems like the way an animal lover would want his favorite pet memorialized, doesn't it?"

About the Center for Great Apes

The Center for Great Apes' mission is to provide a permanent sanctuary for orangutans and chimpanzees who have been retired from the entertainment industry, from research, or who are no longer wanted as pets. The Center provides care with dignity in a safe, healthy, and enriching environment for more than forty great apes in need of lifetime care.

The Center for Great Apes is a 501(c) (3) nonprofit organization, registered with the Florida Department of Agriculture and Consumer Services, # SC-09272 and all contributions are tax deductible as allowed by law. The nonprofit organization was established in 1993 is now located in Wauchula, a small rural community in southern central Florida.

For more info:

Contact:
Phone/fax number:
Email address:

- 0-

Sample Story Pitch

The story pitch is written in a format that does not look like the more traditional press release or media alert, but looks more like a regular email. This is an approach best used when you have confidence that the recipient will open and read your email. Generally speaking, the story pitch format should be used with media people that you have worked with in the past. It is important that you understand and reference a specific audience in your email, to indicate that you understand the program or publication.

In the two examples, you will see that there is some background information given, but slightly less background than you would provide in the electronic media alert format. In this case, my client was willing to provide real time social media response, and that opportunity was included at the end of the story pitch to really round out the value of this story.

Email Subject line: Job Growth at last! Give your viewers the tools they need to land a job of their own!

ATTN NEWS PRODUCERS: Story Idea...

The March Jobless Numbers indicate some real growth on the employment front, so arm your women viewers with the information they need to land a job of their own.

National television personality, author, and motivational speaker Michelle Phillips has put together the do's and the don'ts for winning the job competition in today's difficult workplace environment. In her friendly, conversational style, Michelle shares the tips every job hunter needs to look and feel polished and put together before the big interview.

 In her engaging, fun conversational style, Michelle shares tips and tricks like:

- Dress to Impress—for the important job interview
- Beauty from the Inside Out—what you put in your body, not just on it
- Time Out for You—unplug to recharge your Mind, Beauty, Spirit
- Family Meetings—a fun way to get busy families back on track

- Spring Clean Your Make-up Bag—cheaper is good, but expired is not

These two-minute segments share useful and entertaining tips, making them perfect for your show. The new Michelle Phillips Mind Beauty Spirit segments are available at no charge and can include custom on-air promotion and social media promotion.

For more info:

Contact:
Phone/fax number:
Email address:

More info and demo segments are available for your review at www.mindbeautyspirit.com.

The 3-minute segment can be used in any show, and Michelle will also provide live tweeting and web content promoting your telecast.

- 0 -

Email Subject line: Tax Deadline De-stressor for Your Viewers—A Story Idea

ATTN NEWS PRODUCERS:

The dreaded tax filing day is only 72 hours away, and your viewers need de-stressing tips more than ever. From the lines at the post-office to the backups at H&R Block, this is one of the most stressful weeks of the year.

Renowned working mom and author Michelle Phillips has developed a timely new segment to recharge the mind, the beauty, and the spirit of your viewers. These just-in-time-for-tax-day tips will save time, inspire, and even explain how to " unplug" long enough to lower stress levels. As a sought-after motivational speaker, Michelle has perfected the skills she will share with your viewers to feel better, look better, and be bette . . . even on tax day!

We can make this timely segment available to you immediately!

For more info:

Contact:
Phone/fax number:
Email address:

More information and demo segments are available for your review at www.mindbeautyspirit.com.

The 2-minute segments can be used in any show, and Michelle will also provide live tweeting and web content promoting your telecast.

- 0 -

Sample Interview Prep

Let's turn now to an example of how to prepare for your interview. Chapter 3 details the amount of prep work you must do in advance and to review:

- Be thoroughly versed on every aspect of the story, even the parts that don't pertain to you. Read up, go online, and watch television. Be as expert as you possibly can. Have facts, figures, and details at your fingertips and in your head.

- Being completely up-to-speed on a topic is very, very important. Because you work in the field, you probably know all or most of this information anyway, so it's merely a question of making sure you have the latest and greatest tidbits. Preparation will make your media exposure a home run. A lack of prep will be a death knell for every being invited for another interview.

Let's use one of our earlier story examples of work that a charity is doing for children.

Your story: Your charity is holding a Kid's Fun Day.

Your timely story: With childhood obesity on the rise, exercise for children is more important than ever.

Your preparation: This should include understanding specifically how serious childhood obesity is today. You will need to have this information at your fingertips:

- Approximately how many children are obese today (raw numbers and percentages)? Locally? Regionally? Nationally? Worldwide?
- How has the juvenile obesity problem changed in the last ten years, five years, and two years?
- What do experts think are the primary causes of childhood obesity?
- What first-person experiences do you or your organization have with childhood obesity?
- What is the physical and psychological relationship between childhood obesity and adult obesity?
- Who is most at risk for childhood obesity?
- Why did you get involved in this issue?
- Why did your organization get involved in this issue?
- Who should attend the Kid's Fun Day?

- How will the Kid's Fun Day incorporate exercise into a daylong and lifelong pattern?
- How many people do you expect to attend?
- How can people get additional information?

Sample interview questions:

A good interviewer will already know the answers to most of the questions they ask you, but they need to hear the answers from you. In our sample story the interviewer could also ask you any question like this:

- Do you have any children of your own? Do they suffer from obesity?
- What makes this Fun Day fun?
- What can parents do to help?
- Are you charging money for this event?
- What does it cost to put on an event like this?
- What other events are you planning to address this problem?
- Do you know of any specific families that will be attending?
- Do you do any other kid-focused work?
- Is a one-day event really enough to make a difference in this problem?
- Will you have medical professionals on hand if children experience any problems?
- Are you worried about predators or other threats to children attending this event?

Now before you run screaming from those last two or three questions, you should know that many reporters won't ask these questions, at least not all of them. The bottom line about interview preparation is that you should be able to comfortably answer anything even mildly related to the topic at hand. The original purpose of your event may simply have been "fun for kids," but since you used childhood obesity as your "peg" for news coverage, you have to be prepared to discuss that. Your failure to use a news hook like childhood obesity may mean that the media finds your event too boring to cover at all. Highlighters ready?

> *If you are prepared to answer almost anything, you reduce the risk of being caught off guard. You will look better, smarter, more credible, more trustworthy, and dependable.*

Most reporters are not particularly adversarial. But when you've done so many right things to get as far as an interview, you don't want to risk dropping the ball right before you score the touchdown.

Don't Forget the Follow-up

You will also want to follow up after your interview, to position yourself as a repeat guest or repeat interview possibility. Good steps include:

- Send a very brief email thanking the media person for including you in the story.
- Send a brief email or leave a short voicemail message about the ultimate outcome (number of attendees, number of people who mentioned seeing the story, positive feedback you've received).
- At the first opportunity, contact "your" media person with updated information. Using whatever was the basis for the original story (unemployment, obesity, tax day, Mother's Day, etc.), keep your eyes peeled for new related information and quickly forward that on with an offer to make yourself available to update the story.

Sample Interview Follow-up:

Hi Jim,

Thanks again for the article on the additional hiring at my warehouse. Huge hit with the staff, your reporting made them proud to be working here.

Quick update: Even though the Governor's office announced today that unemployment is rising again, we've added fifteen new workers and plan to hire five more people this month. If you need someone to talk about best ways to get yourself hired in this tough environment I have some great new "do's and don't's" for you.

Call me anytime,
Charlie Michaels
407-123-4567
cgmichaels@juno.com

You're already well on your way to the media coverage you've hoped for! The reason you started hungering for publicity was to turn your company or your event into a success. If you are ready to take advantage of the news coverage you can parlay your increased exposure right into the business growth you need.

Chapter 7

The Main Meal: Taking Advantage of the Publicity

- Turning Visibility into Business
- Turning Credibility into Customers
- Maximize Your Increased Awareness Factor

"Some say opportunity knocks only once, that is not true. Opportunity knocks all the time, but you have to be ready for it. If the chance comes, you must have the equipment to take advantage of it."

—Louis L'Amour

Ever heard that old adage about any publicity being good publicity, as long as they spell your name right? Well, that is fun to say, even pleasant to believe, but not particularly true. The reason most people want publicity is to make money, so to be successful at this process you have to turn increased visibility into increased business.

As a part of debunking the myth, consider this: the theory that any press is good press is patently false, because some publicity is negative (more on that in Chapter 8); but the whole "added exposure" concept is not truly meaningful if it doesn't result in increasing your bottom line. Exposure alone is worthless. You want sales, not exposure. Some PR professionals often say that the phrase "You'll get great exposure" is one of the biggest sucker lines of all times. To be blunt, customers pay the mortgage, media exposure does not. Publicity should equal sales or customers or leads or attendance, and ultimately money in the bank.

What happens when you successfully get yourself that lightning bolt of publicity? How do you make sure that you don't blow the opportunity?

Turning Visibility into Business

Back in Chapter One there was a list of the reasons that press and publicity can be important for you . . . and this is the time to expand on that list. You now know how the media people work. You now know how you will be able to work with the media. Let's map out the final steps:

- Media coverage is the most economical way to reach large audiences—**so that they in turn will want to reach YOU.**
- Publicity can create a strong awareness of and demand for your company products or services—**and you need to be prepared for additional demand.**
- Media exposure helps to develop a positive image for your firm—**so you should quickly capitalize on this more positive change.**
- Studies show that media coverage is five times MORE believable than advertising—**and you must be poised to take advantage of this.**
- The right kind of publicity can turn an ordinary company into a booming business—**provided that you are simultaneously prepared to be a booming enterprise.**

Let's break down the ways that you can and should turn publicity into business:

1. Communicate memorable contact information during the interview
2. Be prepared to succeed
3. Offer specific, usable content in the interview; clearly communicate who needs the information and what they will gain
4. Share the news about your interview externally and internally
5. Share the news about your interview with other media
6. Add a page to your website devoted to your media coverage
7. Measure the success

Although it should go without saying, the first step is very simple and it does relate back to the correct spelling of your name. When you land some press and publicity, you should be certain that your name is spelled correctly, but more importantly that viewers, listeners, or readers also learn a simple way to contact you. Using a **catchy** website (www.healthykids.com) or a **memorable** phone number (1-800-GET-A-JOB) will be worth the time and investment you spend creating it. I spent years coaching advertisers about writing commercial copy and repeatedly counseled them not to include a numeric phone number in their message. The reason? It doesn't work! When was the last time you were watching TV or listening to the radio and you actually wrote down a phone number? Doesn't work in commercials and it doesn't work in interview situations.

When it comes to media coverage, if you don't communicate memorable contact information, you've effectively wasted your time. "Contact information" means your name, phone number, and website. Although I have already detailed that you should not be selling specific products or services in this media environment, your "contact" information is different than outright selling. The principle at play here is that you will be a good, smart, timely, compelling interviewee, and so the audience will want to be able to contact you. Those same people are also your potential customers!

There may be times when gracefully inserting your contact information is impossible, and there will be times when it seems tacky, but if you also successfully work it in to the interview, you will increase your memorability. Here is the first important thing to remember:

> *Erase the word "my" from your vocabulary (as in "my firm", "my company," or even "our event"), and always use the full title to refer to your business or product.*

This is one easy way to reinforce your contact information in an interview without sounding like an infomercial. I continually counsel my clients on this issue, and although they tell me that it feels "weird" at first, they have enjoyed success by doing so. Here are a few examples of how you can make this work without sounding like the proverbial pitchman:

Interview #1

Question: Megan, the heat wave is driving utility bills sky high. What do you suggest that people do to keep cool and keep the cost down?

Your Answer: The two most important things are cooler clothing and drinking plenty of fluids. If you are feeling sick of plain water, just this morning I put a list of the four most hydrating drinks on my website at www.keepyourcool.com to make it easy for people to find.

Interview #2

Question: T.J. you've written a book about college scholarships for athletes, but given the risks aren't you worried about kids getting hurt?

Your Answer: The safety of young athletes is always a primary concern, which is why the first two chapters of *Striking College Gold* are devoted entirely to health and safety. I had a coach tell me last week that he sends his student athletes to collegegold.com specifically because it helps to get their heads on straight about safety.

Interview #3

Question: Mike, the economy is really struggling these days, so what in the world would possess you to build a new factory right now?

Answer: At Buildrite we've done a ton of market research, and we are actually feeling optimistic about the economy here in Florida. As a matter of fact, here is a good video for your readers to check out. Buildrite is so jazzed about this new project that the drivers made their own hilarious music video about it, and it's posted on www.buildritebusinessbuzz all week.

Turning Credibility into Customers

The preparation that your business or organization does prior to the PR is critical. You want your company to be ready when that call comes, so create a scalable infrastructure for your business. In other words, be ready for the increased calls and customers that can arrive in the wake of media attention. Even if the media attention is purely local, you need to be prepared. How your company, organization, receptionist, and team members handle themselves in the spotlight is crucial. And just as important is the ability to quickly ramp up production or service in order to meet any increase in demand. My clients and I actually drill on this aspect, to make positively certain that they are prepared for the potential results of media coverage. Make time for proper timing.

Things can move fast in the media news cycle, and you need to be nimble enough to react. It's nothing short of tragic though when sales—big sales—are lost because of a detail like lack of preparation.

Look at it like this: if you are booking radio or television interviews, give your staff sufficient notice so they have time to work through the supply chain. If you land a national TV interview, you should communicate with your distributor immediately to troubleshoot any inventory issues. Whatever you do, don't let money slip through your fingers because of sloppy preparation.

What your company does to capitalize on publicity determines whether your business grows from obscurity to prominence as a result of the publicity. A completely different kind of preparation is also an important part of the publicity planning process. It is the negative flip side of having a high profile with the news media.

Chapter 8

Make Room for More: How the Media Could Work Against You

- Media Coverage Can Be a Double-edged Sword
- Crisis Control: How To Handle It If You Need It

"I've been getting some bad publicity—but you got to expect that."

—Elvis Presley

This entire book has been devoted to getting press and publicity. You want it, you need it, you deserve it, and you are determined to get it. After following the instructions here, you will have a much better shot at media attention. If we are honest though, not all media attention is positive. And the more you invite the media into your company, your organization, and your life, the greater the chance that you may encounter media coverage that is less-than-positive.

Negative coverage can occur for two reasons:

1. a mistake has been made which comes to the attention of the press
2. a reporter paints you in a negative light

Let's start first with the unlikely scenario that you or an employee have made a mistake, had an unfortunate accident, or misjudged a situation.

Media Coverage Can Be a Double-edged Sword

Lately, a certain celebrity sports figure managed to combine all three of those things, and the result was high-profile, negative, and lengthy media coverage the likes of which we've not seen before. Who? Tiger Woods. No slouch when it comes to golf, Tiger Woods won fourteen major golf tournaments and ranks first in career earnings on the PGA tour. He has also become a notorious media figure.

Was the media coverage warranted? Probably. But the more important questions are: could this have been avoided? How can negative media exposure be kept to a minimum?

Obviously, Tiger's behavior is the kind of story that makes media types salivate. As the tales of the Tiger trysts seemed to grow exponentially, the media had more fodder for every news cycle and deadline. But was the story mostly media hype? His supporters thought so, but I don't agree. Is it possible to be treated with respect instead of with skewering by the media? It can be, if you handle the situation correctly. Tiger Woods simply did not handle it correctly, and that is exactly why the story was not media hype, it was merely a big story.

Let's review what occurred as we work through an example of what **not** to do:

- The original incident was the relatively minor Tiger Woods car crash near Orlando.
- Little was known about the condition of the revered, respected, talented athlete.

- Heavy coverage was journalistically indicated.
- The news coverage was all scaled back when Tiger was released from the hospital later that same day.

So far there had been no harm and no foul on the part of the media. But the story wouldn't die, because Tiger Woods inadvertently fueled the media fire.

> *"A half truth is a whole lie."*
>
> —Yiddish Proverb

Here is a basic tenant of journalism: When a story doesn't make any sense, the reporter should continue to ask questions in order to clarify. So let's look at what happened next:

- Details emerged slowly but regularly, so the story acted like a pendulum swinging back and forth but never fully stopping.
- The official Tiger story of the accident was illogical from the very beginning.
- A petite wife wielding a golf club to rescue her semiconscious husband from the bowels of his Escalade begged more questions.
- Conflicting reports from law enforcement, neighbors, and hospital personnel just didn't add up.
- Women claiming intimate knowledge of Tiger Woods began to come out of the proverbial woodwork because the story stayed in the headlines, which fueled even more headlines.

A vicious media circle. So what can we learn from this? If you have ever landed any media coverage, been interviewed, or are in line to be interviewed, here are five tips that you must remember!

Tip 1: Tell the Truth

Do **not** lie. Do not misrepresent what happened, no matter how foolish you may feel or because you believe you can get away with it. Do not lie. It will not work. The media is nothing if not tenacious. You will be caught in the lie eventually, and the situation will become even worse. Honesty also means: no half truths, no fact fudging, no attempt to misrepresent what has happened. Tell the truth and tell it quickly. If there is a possibility of laws having been broken, consult legal counsel.

Tip 2: Make a Comment

Do **not** refuse to comment, and do not ignore the publicity and the media. In our multimedia, multiplatform world, the negative publicity will not just "go away." Questions will continue and will linger in the minds of the public. Avoidance is a flawed media strategy. Even waiting too long to make a public comment will hurt if you are trying to offset negative perception.

Commenting means "speaking" in the literal sense, as opposed to posting a comment online or issuing a statement through a spokesperson. The failure to comment personally is perceived as cowardly, arrogant, or as a smokescreen, which will compound the negativity you are trying to offset.

Tip 3: Take Your Lumps

Own up to your piece of the problem, including that of your company or your family or your own behavior. An explanation is acceptable, but reacting defensively is not acceptable. Of course, you should not take the blame for things that were genuinely caused by someone else, **but** your failure to see a problem does not excuse you from responsibility. Uncomfortable as it may be in the short term, egregious behavior must be acknowledged if negative press is to be reduced.

Tip 4: Apologize Sincerely

If you are actually sorry for the mistake, you should offer the same heartfelt apology that you would offer a good friend. Phony sounding or non-apology apologies will not cut it when trying to avoid negative publicity.

- A non-apology apology sounds like this: "If you were offended by my actions, then I'm sorry that you felt that way."
- A sincere apology is: "I know that my actions were offensive and I'm very sorry I behaved that way."

Don't even attempt to play the victim card, regardless of how much you may feel like a victim. Customers feel they are owed an apology when their belief system has been undermined.

Tip 5: Be Proactive and Go On the Offensive

To some degree, you may be able to call the shots with your own press conference, press release, online statement, etc. Your ability to respond with sincerity is critical. If you have made a mistake, explain what are going to do to correct it. If you have made an error in judgment or a poor decision, explain the steps you are taking to ensure that it won't happen in the future. You will have to be honest with yourself and with the media about your next steps. But when you are honest, the wind is effectively taken out of the media sail: your story is over and the media is likely to move on to the next story.

Here are some examples of high profile people who better understood the media and were able to deflect at least part of the negative public perception:

- South Carolina Governor Mark Sanford capped off a weekend-long media frenzy by announcing that he had been unfaithful to his wife, had lied to his staff, and had left the country to meet his paramour. His original actions and prevarications aside, Sanford reacted quickly, was honest in his admissions, and was so sincere that he was tearful at his own press conference. He took responsibility for his actions and apologized.

- *Late Night* host David Letterman told his audience that he'd had sex with female members of his staff, and was on the receiving end of an extortion plot. Letterman told the truth, told it in a typically self-deprecating fashion, and vowed proactively to protect his family and his staff.

The bottom line? Bad things do happen, and they can happen to anyone. The media will grab onto a negative story for all it's worth. That is the reality. Bad news sells newspapers and makes people turn on the television. The best advice?

> *Remember that even good people make mistakes. Uncommonly good people react pragmatically and promptly with courage and intelligence.*

As far as media coverage was concerned, Tiger Woods did not respond appropriately:

- His limited statements were disingenuous, and were lacking in credibility because they were completely illogical.
- He would have been more successful mitigating the negative publicity by offering honest revelations early on.
- Failure to respond to growing speculation made the story feed on itself. Press coverage abhors an information vacuum, and the media will actually interview each other if they aren't getting good information from the source.
- In light of what the press had already learned, it was a ludicrous understatement to say, "I am not without faults."
- Serious mistakes in judgment should have been acknowledged as such.

Thomas Jefferson said it best:

> *"Honesty is the first chapter of the book of wisdom."*

This is a very true and important concept in mitigating negative press. It is important not to panic, not to hide, not to shift the blame. This isn't a statement about how you should live your life, only a statement about how to avoid significant negative media coverage. You have worked hard to create a scenario where your business depends on people treating you as a trusted source. With media coverage it takes a long time to gain trust, and a very short time to lose it.

Crisis Control: How to Handle It If You Need It

Sometimes negative coverage occurs through absolutely no fault of your own. You agreed to an interview and communicated the information that was important. But the journalist has misrepresented you, misquoted you, or slanted the story in a way that you did not anticipate. What should you do in this case?

Before you leap into action, it is a good idea to check with one or two trusted sources and make sure they agree that you appear in a bad light. Sometimes our own perception and reality are slightly out of synch. But if your allies agree that the story was negative, then you can take the following steps:

- **Develop a thicker skin.** As the saying goes, "If you can't run with the big dogs, you've gotta stay on the porch." This is the risk/reward ratio that we alluded to in the very beginning of the book. In my experience, the reward outweighs the risk; but the risk exists nonetheless.

- **Contact the news reporter and copy their supervisor.** If the story is factually incorrect or unduly biased, most media will issue corrections for factual errors. Don't, however, expect the reporter to do an immediate Follow-up Story, or expect the correction to be in the same fashion as the original story. Generally speaking, this just doesn't happen.

- **Be objective.** Even though you are not feeling calm, you should remain professional. You should not assume that the mistakes were deliberate.

- After contacting the reporter, wait at least two working days for a response. Even if a reporter has already crafted their response to you, they will have to clear it with management.

- **Issue a public response.** Sometimes bad press can damage your reputation, so it may be necessary to issue a public response. Sending a straightforward news release offers the most efficient means of disseminating the corrected information. You can also consider an online response and share your side of the story with the rest of the world.

- **Decide not to take action.** While inaction seems lame and weak, remember the news cycles aren't very long, and bad press can fade quickly. Weigh the importance or the degree of severity before you decide. Responding publicly can train an even harsher spotlight on the issue.

There may be times when you are thrust into a crisis control situation, so I'd like to impart some tips about handling the media under unpleasant circumstances. My tips were earned and learned the hard way while managing my way through news coverage of:

- a television news producer secretly posing for a *Playboy* cover shot while lying nude across my station news desk

- unfortunate video of a nudist camp that managed to make its way into my nightly newscast

- a robbery and shooting of the morning news anchor while on her way into the television station

So I really do have some experience with negative publicity, and I suggest that **first of all** you take a deep breath. If a crisis becomes public knowledge and the media becomes involved, you will need to monitor media coverage closely. The coverage will increase public awareness by informing your customers all at once, and day after day. The media tends to see itself as a watchdog. One news director who worked for me frequently referred to her team of reporters as "giving voice to the voiceless." With a mindset like that, you will need to keep your wits about you. Like it or not, the media makes judgments about you based on how you respond to their emergency calls.

Once the crisis reaches the newspapers and television, act quickly. Even though it would be your preference (it was mine too) to wait for complete information, it is better to meet with the media sooner rather than later, or at least offer to do so. You should address questions as best you can and then offer to report back when you have further information. As we discussed in Chapter 1, newspapers have deadlines; television stations broadcast their stories before dinner; and online news never stops. So your reluctance to give your point of view within the media's time frame means the day's stories will one-sided.

Whether a negative situation was thrust upon you by outside variables or you had a hand in creating the problem, there are some truisms that will drive most people crazy about media coverage in a crisis situation:

- The media has a much louder voice than you do, combined with an audience perception that, "If I saw it on the news, it must be true."

- "Off the record" and "no comment" work much better in the movies than in real life. I personally think that "off the record" only works if the reporter feels like adhering to your request, and unfortunately saying "no comment" just makes you sound guilty.

- A reporter can challenge anything you say, but historically that process is a one-way street. When you try to challenge that reporter it will not work. Trust me.

- If you treat the media like your enemy, they will be your enemy.

- You cannot assume that "truth will triumph," because by the time it does your credibility is too damaged. You can't disregard the notion that perception is as damaging as reality—sometimes more so.
- You cannot assume that your reputation will speak for itself. Two words: Tiger Woods.
- You cannot offer the media written statements only. Yes, it's a lot easier to communicate via written statements but it's impersonal and arrogant-sounding, and people think it means you're hiding something. See those two words again!

Crisis Survivability Means:

- Correct all factual errors promptly, and if you can't solve the problem right away, provide as much information as is available. This will reassure the media that you are at least interested in their concerns and questions.
- Be proactive and not reactive.
- Use language and terminology that the public will understand; industry jargon makes you sound like you are trying to hide something.
- Address the emotion of the crisis as well as the facts of the crisis.

Remember the wise saying, "This too shall pass." Successful people like you know that calculated risks are part of doing business. The risk of negative media coverage is lower than the risk of **no** media coverage: the former is unpleasant, but the latter can mean no business growth, and ultimately the end of your business.

The rewards of press and publicity can be tremendous. Let's do a final review of the process from soup to nuts.

Chapter 9

I Can't Believe I Ate the Whole Thing: A Final Review and Recap of Publicity

- Summary
- Inspirational words

"When you do the common things in life in an uncommon way, you will command the attention of the world."

—George Washington Carver

When you picked up this book and started reading the early chapters, getting yourself press and publicity was an unknown. As a small business owner, doctor, dentist, attorney, realtor, financial consultant, software developer, business consultant, career counselor, educator, or manager at a nonprofit organization, you now have the information you need to crack the code on getting yourself some media attention. I use this same material very strategically for my own clients every day. Without a deep background in communications or media, you are now armed with more insider information than you can shake a television remote at! Let's do a recap of the most important elements.

The Good Things That Media Attention Can Do For You

Exposure in the media is very desirable because it so powerful. The message reaches many people simultaneously, regardless of whether you appear in a trade publication or on national television. It is nearly impossible to reach so many people at one time without help from the media.

Media coverage creates awareness of your name, your expertise, your opinion, your brand, your business, or your event. By understanding the power of media coverage, you can rocket from anonymity to household status quickly. From political pundit Joe the Plumber to singing sensation Susan Boyle to airline pilot hero Sully Sullenberger, the media can put you in the fame fast lane.

Press and publicity is certainly an economical communication vehicle. Some people call press coverage "free advertising," and although it doesn't have a specific price tag, you shouldn't think of it as completely free either. Media coverage does cost less money than purchasing advertising time or space, BUT it requires your prep time, planning, organizing, and vigilance to secure coverage. I'm a big believer that your time and brain power are worth something. Maybe not the dollars and sense of an ad buy, but not free either. Regardless of how you look at it, though, news media coverage is economical and can drive huge value to your bottom line.

On a related economic note, media coverage blankets you with a credibility that you simply cannot buy. The audience perceives that an interview means that the reporter endorses you and your story. The credibility factor really makes the entire media attention process worth it to many people just like you, and it doesn't cost a cent!

And because of the power of media exposure, you will have dramatically increased visibility with your customers, your potential customers, your competitors, your shareholders, and even your own staff. Your media exposure feels organic to consumers—organic meaning that you didn't buy advertising or force an interview to happen. (We will just keep all of your behind-the-scenes work our little secret.)

And as we just noted, the credibility factor of media coverage positions you as an expert in your field. After all, if the media comes to you for information and insight, then you MUST be an expert. Right? Right!

And even after the initial blush of media attention, your exposure will reinforce the strength of your name or your business. Media coverage is great brand reinforcement.

You Can Become A Media Heavyweight by Using the FAT Method

I'm sure you remember that the catchy FAT acronym stands for:

- Focused
- Attention-grabbing
- Timely

Being focused in the FAT method means simply that your media alert should be tightly focused on **one** thing. Do not cram several pieces or tidbits of info into the press release no matter how interesting you personally may find those things. To a media person, if you are unfocused in your story approach, that will translate to you being an unfocused interviewee, a potentially disorganized guest who will be late for the broadcast, and worst of all someone who will not be able to speak in good shorts bursts of useable information.

Focus also means giving consideration to the best media for your particular story. A broad and even more compelling announcement must be crafted to reach the national media and even local mass media like local TV and newspapers, so use your focus to cut your publicity teeth. Successfully getting media coverage on a small or local scale leads to bigger and better publicity in the future.

Focus on getting the biggest bang for your communication buck. Trade publications can be the perfect and most effective vehicle in many cases, even if they are not as sexy as *The Today Show*.

After you master the focus thing, you can concentrate on grabbing attention. When you sit down to craft an announcement for the news media, it is vital that it be attention-grabbing, or else your announcement is on the fast track to the delete button. The headline you use will either make or break your story when it comes to grabbing attention.

When attempting to get publicity in the news media, you are only communicating with a single reporter, or one editor, or an individual producer, and since you have an audience of one it will be easier for you to be attention-grabbing.

A Good *Headline* Sells the Reporter Into Wanting to Find Out More By Reading or Hearing What Comes Next

- Headlines should be less than two lines and summarize the announcement
- Tell your "story" in a one sentence headline
- Make the sentence active and interesting
- Complete sentences are not necessary
- Don't put a proper name in your headline
- Write or rewrite the headline last

Remember too that media coverage waits for no man. You've got to be prepared to move quickly so that you will be timely. This is the last and most complex aspect of the FAT method of press and publicity. Since publicity is opportunistic it means that your timing is everything. Creating a timely announcement means positioning your news announcement as relevant and current. This becomes easier with practice, but as a starting point you should consider what is going on around you locally, regionally, nationally, and industry-wise, so you can relate that to your story.

You Should Be Prepared to Act Quickly and You Must Seize the Day—the Window for Being 'TRULY TIMELY' Is Short

The perfect press and publicity opportunity may open suddenly and can snap shut just as quickly. In addition to regular seasonal events, holidays, and longer lasting socioeconomic trends, big news and weather events will suddenly occur. The people who are able to react and act quickly will be the publicity beneficiaries.

When I sat down to summarize the FAT method, I was simultaneously emailing an author client of mine about a timely opportunity. This particular author had just finished a book about race relations, which was also a subject that had mired a well-known radio talk show host in controversy within the last thirty-six hours. I counseled the author that it was hugely important to send out her own media alert immediately. The author politely pointed out that since it was a Saturday she would prefer to take the day off. Would you like to guess what my next message was? Take a look:

From: Sandi

To: XXX

Subject: you need to move quickly on this…

Hey XXXX,

What is this "resting today" that you speak of? LOL! Seriously, it is NOT too late today, but I wouldn't wait much longer. This is exactly what I meant about timely media opportunities. We have to keep our ears to the ground so we don't miss 'em and we have to move quickly. It hardly ever happens at a convenient time!

Sandi

This real life exchange illustrates the timely opportunity you may have, but also the challenges of being timely.

The beauty of the FAT method of press and publicity is that it will work for you specifically because it will work for the news media. Since you understand what the media needs, you can offer that to them, and you will begin to get press and publicity exposure.

FAT works because:

- your **FOCUS** will be noted and appreciated
- your **ATTENTION GRABBING** will do just that
- being **TIMELY** will position you to supply unique, fresh angles of news story context

You get what you need. The media gets what they need. FAT and happy!

We Are Gathered Here Today to Say Goodbye to the Standard Press Release

You may have noticed that you've not read the words "press release" since Chapter 2. The reason is that the standard old press release has gone toes up. This is the era of the **Media Alert.** The FAT method definitely applies but should be used electronically and orally only. Do **not** send faxes and do **not** snail mail a press release. The reasons are simple:

- speed matters
- being perceived as contemporary and current is important
- media people are almost exclusively focused on computer and mobile devices when newsgathering

Media Contacts and Approach Style

Chapter 3 was all about the need to know the media outlet you are approaching, understanding the distribution method and knowing their target audience. You will need to do some detective work to get the correct names and email addresses, and once you are clear on those things you can approach the media in this manner:

Television

News Director, Vice President of News, or President of News
Assignment Editor
News Anchor, Show Host
Producer
Reporter

Radio

News Director
Producer
News Anchor, Show Host, On-air Personality

Newspaper

Features Editor
Assistant Editor
News Editor
Reporter
Columnist

Print magazines

Publisher
Editor
Reporter

Online magazines

Editor

Writer

There are also services which large companies use to supply all of the names and addresses, but those services are pricey and designed for experienced users who already know the title of the best person to contact. I use them for some of my clients but not all of them, because a little time spent online researching your media target will typically yield you good results. Remember, too, that it is important that you have your media pitch well-focused when you contact the media.

After You Get Some Media Arranged, Here is How to Prevent a Case of Cold Feet!

Tips I suggest are to relax and adhere to the drills that work well for my clients:

1. Rehearse the basic points you want to make **out loud**.
2. Take a few deep breathes and then speak more slowly than you normally would.
3. For in-person interviews, look the interviewer **in the eyes.**
4. If you don't know the answer, simply say that you don't have an answer.
5. Be thoroughly versed on every aspect of the story, even the parts that don't pertain to you.

Media Appearance Preparation

Prior to media exposure, it is super-important that you be completely up-to-speed on your topic. Read up, go online, watch television, and be as expert as you possibly can. Have facts, figures, and details at your fingertips and in your head. Preparation will make your media exposure a home run.

Among a long list of good reasons to be thoroughly prepped, you will feel more confident, and being more confident will make you a better interviewee. You may have the opportunity to work some of this information into the interview and increase your own credibility as a trusted expert. Your media contact will be impressed and make a mental note that you are a good source for this type of information.

Great pre-interview preparation will clearly demonstrate that you are an expert in your field. The media will take note, and consumers will take note too.

Set Good Publicity Goals

Remember that your press and publicity efforts should be a well-thought-out process. Focus on the people you want to reach—who they are, where they are, and which media will best help you reach them. Resource allocation is an important considera-tion, and you need to be clear on your goals before you can be clear on the resources you will need.

Media Strategy

A media strategy is the specific route you plan to take in order to achieve your publicity goals. Strategy is really the mechanics of planning. Brand awareness, reputation, and your bottom line can all affected by media coverage.

A media strategy is simply a plan. A concise plan. A media strat-egy is a tool to help you focus your publicity and press coverage efforts. Choose a media strategy that is in perfect synch with your business and marketing goals and sets you apart from your competition. To do this, keep your eye on the big picture and develop adequate systems for dealing with the media. And as we discussed in a number of areas, the more planning you get done in advance, the more effective your media work will be. You should know your communication strengths and weaknesses, and you should also decide how you want to be perceived by the media and by potential customers.

Is there a negative way the media could present you or your event? Think through the ramifications and possible avoidance tactics.

Advertising Is Not All Bad

I do **not** believe that advertising is a bad thing. There is room in a good media strategy for both publicity and advertising, and these can complement each other. The value of advertising is that **you** can totally control the message, but in an interview you have very limited control over the message. Advertising can and should explain the specific features and benefits of a product, and can also provide information that helps consumers make an informed buying decision. Your press and publicity plan will not allow you to sell anything directly, but advertising allows you to unabashedly tell and sell the world!

The ICCK Approach to Story Pitches

My key to crafting an effective message to send to the media is the ICCK factor. In this approach, ICCK stands for Imagination, Creativity, Curiosity, and Knowledge.

As I mentioned earlier, the fact that you are reading this book means that you can already use your imagination to see possibility that others can't. So it won't be too much of a stretch to apply some creative, outside-the-box thinking to a media pitch topic. The process can become easier with practice. So start practicing creativity regularly as soon as you can.

Curious people ask questions and search for answers. When you are curious about something, your mind expects and anticipates new ideas. By being curious, you will be able to see new possibilities which are invisible to other people. It takes a curious mind to look beneath the surface and discover new possibilities. And as you know now, there are simply tons of press and publicity possibilities for you!

It is important, too, that while you are contemplating press and publicity, you stay current and knowledgeable about your own industry and the events going on around town and around the world. You may or may not be a person who regularly watches television news, reads newspapers, or gets news online. But you'll find that it is worthwhile to devote yourself to this task when it comes to media alerts.

Maximizing Media to the Max

You and I aren't spending all of this time and effort to get press and publicity attention just to feed our own ego. The reason you want publicity is to make money, so to be successful at this process you have to turn increased visibility into increased business. Publicity should equal sales or customers or leads or attendance, and ultimately money in the bank.

The ways that you can turn publicity into business include:

1. Communicate memorable contact information
2. Be prepared to succeed
3. Offer specific, usable content in the interview; clearly communicate who needs the information and what they will gain
4. Share the news about your interview externally and internally
5. Share the news about your interview with other media
6. Measure the success

And last but not least:

How to Avoid the Media Quicksand and Quagmire

When you open yourself up to the possibility of press coverage, you also unfortunately open yourself up to potentially negative consequences. The two ways this can happen are through a mistake of yours, or a mistake made by the reporter.

In the event that you have created the problem yourself remember:

- Do not lie
- Do make a comment
- Take your lumps
- Apologize sincerely
- Be proactive

On the flip side, if you've been painted unfairly with a negative report you will need to choose the right way to respond. Your options will include:

- Develop a thicker skin
- Contact the news reporter and copy their supervisor
- Be objective
- After contacting the reporter, wait for at least two working days for a response
- Issue a public response
- Take no action

This is the risk/reward ratio that we mentioned in the very beginning of the book. In my experience, the reward outweighs the risk, but the risk exists nonetheless.

Conclusion

Media exposure and publicity is a powerful weapon, regardless of who you are or what you do. Media coverage can mean that you are perceived as having expertise that other people don't have. This expertise or so-called credibility makes you more valuable to potential customers.

The media is full of opportunities, and good publicity can cast you in a positive light. The glow of great press can grow your bottom line. Consumers are bombarded with nonstop commercial messages, so noncommercial media coverage can set you apart.

Publicity is not a *battle* to be fought. Publicity is an intelligent *partnership*. It has its own rules—and now you have a copy of the rulebook!

Finally, you should treat publicity like a relationship to be nurtured. When I work with my brethren in the media I like to paraphrase one of my favorite quotes:

> *"The media people may forget what you said but they will never forget how you made them feel."*

Appendix

- Nuts and Bolts (or as I like to say, "Blah, blah, blah")

Unless you are a media geek like I am, this is pretty boring stuff. But it is still good, though, to know the differences and similarities between local, national, broadcast, cable, and satellite media. If you aren't particularly media savvy right now, after reading this final section of the book you will be the life of the next cocktail party with your smart insights! More importantly you will know why some PR folks get paid the big bucks.

Local media

Local television news: is produced at television stations that are physically located in or near your metropolitan area. Television stations always have "call letters," which are the 4 letters that are used to identify them to the FCC and these always start with a W or a K. WXYZ or KABC for example. As a viewer you may not ever hear those letters. That is because some crafty television stations also use catchy slogans to identify themselves to viewers. You be more familiar with Eyewitness News, ABC 7, Channel 9 News, FOX 5, 10@10 and many, many other variations. Knowing the call letters will be helpful initially, because when you Google the station or look it up in the phone book, you need to have a place to start. Knowing your p's and q's will help you. . .actually when it comes to local TV, knowing your W's and K's will help you!

Local television stations: are frequently owned by larger broadcast companies that are located in a faraway city. By law, a company can own two television stations in a given town, but not any more than that. One more note about local TV: there are basically two different kinds of television stations: the ones that produce news (sometimes called "network affiliates"), and those that only run entertainment programming like sitcom reruns, talk shows, court shows, etc.

Local radio stations: operate much the same way as Local TV stations. Call letters, licenses from the federal government, often owned by large companies, cute catchy names like Magic 105, Smooth Jazz 98.7, News Talk 580. There are two frequencies that radio stations can operate on and which you probably know from using your car stereo: FM and AM. But there are also important differences between radio and television:

1. one company may own up to eight radio stations in one city
2. radio stations have much smaller staffs and operating budgets than most television stations

Local cable news: is produced by the company that owns the cable television franchise in your city. Your cable operator may be a large company like Time Warner, Cox, or Comcast, or it may be a smaller cable operator. In cities that are large enough to make it financially viable, the cable company often runs a local news channel. Think CNN, but dedicated to stories in your town. When you watch TV, this Local Cable Channel looks exactly like a television station. The difference is that viewers who subscribe to cable TV are the only people can see it. On average, about 70% of the population in a city has cable.

Are you eyes drooping from boredom yet? I know this information seems pretty dry. But as you head down a path of securing media coverage, you will be much more successful if you've taken a tiny bit of time to understand how the media business works. This approach is the same kind of strategic approach that you would apply to your own business. The devil is in the details.

A quick case in point: while running a **National Television News** show I was often pitched a story by well-meaning PR flacks. These PR pro's would begin their proposal for news coverage with the words, "Now, this is a local radio show, right?" **Wrong!** I didn't have the time, energy, or patience to listen to someone who hadn't even bothered to figure out what kind of media I represented. You wouldn't go the dentist and ask him to take a look at your tennis elbow! You wouldn't call a CPA about a computer software problem! Same thing.

Print people: this would be the daily newspaper, a weekly newspaper and local magazines. Daily newspapers are often owned by the same type of large media companies that own radio and television stations. Weekly newspapers and the local magazines are generally owned locally, by someone who lives in or nearby the same city. Electronic media in all forms will be seen or heard by more people than most print publications.

National Coverage

Understanding national (morning and nightly) news broadcasts requires that you know just a tiny bit about how a national network works and its relationship to your local television stations.

Television networks are: large for-profit companies that have an agreement with local television stations in different cities. The specific agreement can vary, but typically the local station agrees to give up part of each day to broadcast all of the network shows (soap operas, national news in the morning and in the early evening, and prime time entertainment shows like *Grey's Anatomy*, *Lost*, *NCIS*, *Law and Order*, and big sporting events).

Based on the time zone you live in, the entire country sees the same network shows at the same time. Both the station and the network sell commercials in these programs, and each gets to keep whatever money they make from advertisers.

Still with me? In most cities you will find at least three or four local TV stations, each working with a different network. The national news produced by the network and the local news produced by the station have virtually nothing in common. By that I mean that the staffing is different, the presenters are different, the focus of the show is different, and the budgets are hugely different.

Network news: is produced out of the national network offices in New York City, which is also where you can find the majority of the writing and producing staff.

Remember what we said about everyone in the country seeing the network news at the same time? This is the BIG advantage for national and network media coverage, because you can get tons of people watching you by appearing on national TV only once. There are two big downsides to national news:

1. It is much more difficult to get national media coverage than it is to get local media coverage

2. The people who work in the national media tend to be very savvy and may ask you much more difficult questions, questions you are not prepared for, and even questions you would prefer not to discuss

National (syndicated) radio: is built along the same lines as television networks. The national radio shows air on local radio stations that have turned part of their day and airwaves over to the national voice. This category would include programs that feature Glenn Beck, Rush Limbaugh, John Tesh, Tom Joyner, Sean Hannity, Garrison Keillor, Steve Harvey, Don Imus, and Howard Stern. The same selling-of-advertising model also applies: both the national people and the local people get to sell the airtime and keep whatever they sell. The advantage of doing one interview and having it heard round the country is another similarity to national television.

National daily newspapers are: this country's biggest newspapers, including *The New York Times*, *USA Today*, and *The Wall Street Journal*. Although their readership has declined right along with your local newspaper, the bigger and meatier budgets that they have mean that they are now becoming quite strong online. An article in any of these publications may be read online instead of on paper, and this effectively extends the reach of the national newspapers.

National cable news network's are: best described as a hybrid of the other news media we've discussed. They are not available to all viewers, but instead to the people who subscribe to cable television in their individual towns.

Being interviewed or talked about on one of the national cable news shows can have the same benefit of large one-time-only exposure for you, with for two caveats:

- First, the number of people who watch these channels is actually much lower than you would expect. This low number of viewers is caused by the fact that they are only on cable television, that they carry news twenty-four hours a day, and that there are so many viewing options for people to choose from.
- Secondly, the news viewing public believes that broadcast television news is more credible than national cable news.

According to biannual studies conducted by the Television Bureau of Advertising and Nielsen Media Research, the public consistently perceives broadcast television as the most influential, most authoritative, most exciting, and most persuasive advertising medium. Despite the attention given to cable news networks such as FOX News and CNN, broadcast TV such as NBC, ABC and CBS are consistently seen as the primary news source, the first choice for weather and traffic and sports, and the most involved in community.

One of the little secrets news media insiders understand is that working for or being interviewed on the cable news channels *seems* impressive, but in reality the cable network and your story may be seen by only a small number of people. In many cities, one story on a popular local television news show is actually seen by more viewers than the same story on an entire cable news network.

Here is a brief overview of the cable television news organizations:

> MSNBC and CNBC: owned and operated by General Electric (who also owns the NBC Television Network)

> FOX News Channel: owned by Rupert Murdoch (who also owns the *New York Post*)

> Bloomberg: owned by Michael Bloomberg

> CNN and Headline News: owned by Time Warner (who also owns *TIME* Magazine)

> ESPN and ESPN II: owned by the Disney Corporation (who also owns the ABC Television Network)

For More Information

If you have questions about anything covered in *Breaking Your Own News,* or if you are looking for professional assistance with publicity, press, media, or writing, please do not hesitate to contact me. I am happy to answer your question, and I can also provide a number of publicity related services, including:

- Publicity consultation
- Media alert writing
- Social media consultation
- Interview preparation
- Publicity goal setting
- Audience analysis
- Media coaching
- Publicity critiquing and evaluation
- On-site Media 101 seminars
- On-site Publicity Basics seminars

Please let me know how I can help you break your own news.

Sandra Gehring
email: gehring123@gmail.com
www.sandragehring.com
www.breakingyourownnews.com

About the Author

SANDI GEHRING is a publicity consultant who specializes in getting her clients favorable media coverage on national TV, talk radio, newspapers, and the Internet. She lends her clients twenty-five years of experience working for companies such as CNN, NBC, CNBC Asia, the *New York Times*, and *The Daily Buzz*. Sandi has won an Emmy for writing and producing a broadcast multi-media public service campaign. She is the author of *The Complete Guide to Marketing and Selling to the Affluent: Everything You need to Know to Attract and Keep Wealthy Customers*. She lives in Florida with her husband and children. She is currently raising a future NFL linebacker.